QUEEN ELIZABETH II

TIMES BOOKS

Published by Times Books

An imprint of HarperCollins Publishers
Westerhill Road, Bishopbriggs
Glasgow G64 2QT

HarperCollins Publishers
1st Floor, Watermarque Building,
Ringsend Road, Dublin 4, Ireland

First edition 2021
Second edition 2022

A catalogue record for this book is available
from the British Library.

ISBN 978-0-00-858148-0

10 9 8 7 6 5 4 3 2 1

Printed in Bosnia and Herzegovina

Thanks and acknowledgements go to Joanne Lovey and
Robin Ashton at News Syndication and, in particular,
at The Times, Ian Brunskill and Nigel Farndale and,
at HarperCollins, Rachel Allegro, Beth Ralston,
Jethro Lennox, Harley Griffiths, Kevin Robbins,
Keith Moore and Elizabeth Donald.

This book is produced from independently certified
FSC™ paper to ensure responsible forest management.

For more information visit: www.harpercollins.co.uk/green

THE TIMES

QUEEN ELIZABETH II

COMMEMORATING HER LIFE AND REIGN 1926 – 2022

Edited by
James Owen

CONTENTS

8 Introduction

13 BORN TO SERVE

14 *Birth of a Princess*

16 A Royal Childhood

28 *King Edward's Farewell*

30 A Princess at War

38 *Princess Elizabeth, Preparation for Future Responsibilities*

42 *Night Scenes in London, Royal Family on Palace Balcony, Rejoicing Crowds*

47 A PRINCESS IN LOVE

48 "How high he can jump!"

58 *Marriage of Princess Elizabeth. The Ceremony in the Abbey.*

64 His Own Man

70 Strength and Stay

81 I VOW TO THEE, MY COUNTRY

82 Long Live the Queen

84 *Death of the King*

88 The Light Shines in the Darkness

90 The Coronation

96 *The Queen Crowned at Westminster*

101 HEAD OF STATE

102 Her Majesty's Governments

116 The Quiet Diplomat

132 56 Countries, 92 Languages: The Commonwealth

143 QUEEN AND COUNTRY

144 The Crown

150 *Peace Returns to Aberfan, Villagers Moved by Queen's Visit*

152 The Royal Garden Party

156 Fit for a Queen

169 RULING PASSIONS

170 The Queen at Home

176 A Queen's Best Friends

182 Sport of Queens

191 A FAMILY AFFAIR

192 The Royal Triumvirate

198 The Queen's Children

210 The Queen and Diana

215 A NEW ELIZABETHAN AGE

216 A True Annus Horribilis

220 *The Queen Shares Her Sadness*

224 Reinventing the Monarchy

236 Just Granny

244 The Future: George, Charlotte & Louis

248 *A Prince's Repose*

254 After Philip

265 END OF A REIGN

266 *Queen Elizabeth II dies*

270 Queen Elizabeth II obituary

324 *Queen is laid to rest with splendour and pageantry*

332 A Hard Act to Follow

"I declare before you all that my whole life whether it be long or short shall be devoted to your service..."

The Queen, April 21, 1947

INTRODUCTION
by James Owen

There were few other presences in most people's lives as constant as the Queen. Britain's longest-reigning monarch was our sovereign for 70 years and famous for almost 100. She was as much a part of our culture as red post boxes, as familiar as cloudy skies and as reassuring as tea and toast. And yet, what did we really know about her?

A century ago, when she was born, such a question would not have been asked. The press, like everyone else, knew their place. The royal family was at the top of society, indeed at the top of a world in which Britain, with an empire covering a quarter of the globe, was still the dominant power.

With ever-gathering speed, that world changed forever during Elizabeth's reign. She was at the centre of extraordinary events, not least in her own family, for decade after decade. And yet, she weathered them.

More than most, she had to adapt herself to a different way of doing things. The outer splendour of her life may have appeared to remain much the same, but during her years on the throne the monarchy had to renegotiate its relationship with its subjects. It had to accept far greater scrutiny of its privileges and much more curiosity about the behaviour of those who enjoy them.

The Queen, however, with very few exceptions, never lost her standing with her people; it would have been impossible to think of her, unlike Queen Victoria, being booed in public. Always on show, never saying anything controversial – indeed hardly anything truly memorable – she allowed few glimpses of what she actually thought or felt.

She was simply there, and we are rightly grateful for her decades of unstinting service and for the stability she provided. But she was an enigma.

As we mourn her passing, as what were key moments in both her life and ours turn from news into history, this volume both preserves her remarkable achievements and seeks to understand how she came to accomplish them.

If the photographs provide a comprehensive record of her public life, the selection of short essays by writers at *The Times* and by leading royal historians, interspersed with contemporary news reports on turning points in her life, offer a series of perspectives on the less visible Queen – the private experiences and inner qualities that shaped her and her reign.

Her path to the throne was extraordinary just in itself. When she was born, in 1926, there was no expectation that she would become Queen, as her father, then the Duke of York, was the younger brother of the heir, the future King Edward VIII. With her uncle's abdication in 1936, her world, and that of her parents and her sister, Princess Margaret, was turned upside down.

Like ordinary Britons, she endured the war years, served in the armed forces as a driver, and even escaped briefly from Buckingham Palace to take part in the jubilation of VE Day. Her choice of husband was similarly bold, for Prince Philip was, by royal standards, an outsider and a foreigner, with few prospects and a maverick, modernising streak.

Nevertheless, he gave her the support she needed when she succeeded to the throne at 25, in 1952, and provided much of the impetus for the changes needed to fit the institution of monarchy to a new world. The essays detail the Queen's relationships with the prime ministers who served her, beginning with Winston Churchill, her influence on diplomatic relations with countries such as America, and her dedicated leadership of a Commonwealth which now encompasses 56 different nations.

What sustained her all that time, beyond her profound sense of duty, were her enthusiasms, notably horse racing and her beloved dogs, her homes, and her family – her parents, her children and the grandchildren and great-grandchildren who now will follow her.

Together with her shrewd choice of advisers, they enabled her in the last 20 years to transform faster than ever the shape of the monarchy, recognising the public discontent that met the official reaction to the death of Diana, Princess of Wales, and rebuilding, too, from the ashes of the fire-ravaged Windsor Castle.

For all the pageantry and ceremony with which we associate the Queen in her public role, what underpinned this was her personal modesty, the sense that she never took things for granted. How fortunate we were to have her all those years.

The Queen at the Royal Windsor Cup, July 2021.

BORN
TO SERVE

∼ Birth of a Princess ∼

The Court Circular issued from Windsor Castle last night opens with the following paragraph: The King and Queen have received with great pleasure the news that the Duchess of York gave birth to a daughter this morning. Their Majesties had been awakened between 3 and 4 a.m. to receive the news of the birth of their first grand-daughter. No. 17, Bruton street, where the Duke and Duchess recently went to reside temporarily, is the London residence of the Earl and Countess of Strathmore, the parents of the Duchess of York, who had been staying in London in view of the expected birth of the child.

In accordance with custom where births in the royal family are concerned, the Home Secretary, Sir William Joynson-Hicks, had been summoned to Bruton street, and he was present in the house at the time of the birth. In accordance with custom also the Home Secretary conveyed to the Lord Mayor by special messenger the intimation of the birth of the Princess. The announcement and the subsequent bulletin were posted outside the Mansion House. To a telegram from the Mansion House, the Duke of York sent the following reply to the Lord Mayor: "Please accept and convey to the citizens of London our sincere thanks for their kind congratulations, which we deeply appreciate. The Duchess and baby are making excellent progress.-ALBERT."

The Times, April 22, 1926

The Duke and Duchess of York with their daughter, Princess Elizabeth.

A ROYAL CHILDHOOD
by Kate Williams

On December 10, 1936, the ten-year-old Princess Elizabeth of York was at home at No. 145 Piccadilly with her sister, Margaret. Preparing to write up her notes from her swimming lesson, she heard shouts of "God save the King" from outside. She realised that people were calling for her father. She asked a footman the reason for the noise. He told her – and she dashed straight up the stairs to Margaret. "Uncle David is going away and isn't coming back, and Papa is going to be King."

"Does that mean you will have to be the next Queen?" demanded Margaret, only six.

"Yes, some day," said her sister. "Poor you," replied Margaret.

Elizabeth was unruffled. As she would do throughout her life at moments of crisis, she maintained her routine. According to the diary of her governess, Marion Crawford, she sat down and began to write up her notes from the swimming lesson. She wrote at the top of the paper: Abdication Day.

Elizabeth Alexandra Mary was born in the early hours of April 21, 1926, at 17 Bruton Street in Mayfair, the home of her mother's family. She was immediately everybody's favourite. "We have long wanted a child to make our happiness complete," wrote her father, Albert, or "Bertie", Duke of York. The King and Queen, stiff and even unforgiving with their own children, were delighted by their "little darling", who was third in line to the throne at birth. She was named after her mother, great-grandmother and grandmother-consorts rather than queens regnant.

"He says nothing about Victoria," George V reported of his son. "I hardly think it necessary." In other words, the princess didn't need the name of the great female monarch because she would never be Queen.

Although never intended to reign, little "Lilibet" was catapulted into the full glare of media attention. One newspaper dubbed her "the world's best-known baby". "It almost frightens me that the people love her so much," said her mother, the Duchess of York. "I hope she will be worthy of it." However, the princess was most cherished by the King. She called him "Grandpa England".

When Margaret was born, in Scotland in August 1930, Elizabeth was thrilled. "I have got a new baby sister," she told an estate tenant. "She is so very lovely." The Yorks were now "we four" or "us four", surprisingly close for the aristocratic standards of the time, giggling together at bedtime in their new Piccadilly home. The property was huge – with a lift and a ballroom – but it was a house, rather than a palace. Elizabeth and Margaret played in the gardens with the daughters of the neighbours – businessmen and doctors, rather than royals. The two sisters were cared for by the nannies Clara Knight and Margaret (or "Bobo") MacDonald, who kept them to a strict routine of meals, naps and airings.

The sisters played very different roles in the family. Elizabeth was conscientious, striving, dutiful – and so orderly that she couldn't sleep if her shoes were not parallel under her bed. Margaret was spirited and naughty – as she grew older, she blamed every fault on her invented "Cousin Halifax". The duke remarked on Elizabeth's perfectionism and indulged Margaret's silly games.

The duchess wanted her daughters to have "a really happy childhood … and later, happy marriages". She was not a believer in too much education. The duke had been bullied at school and agreed to a light timetable. All King George wished for was that they develop a "decent hand" – because, he said, "none of my children could write properly".

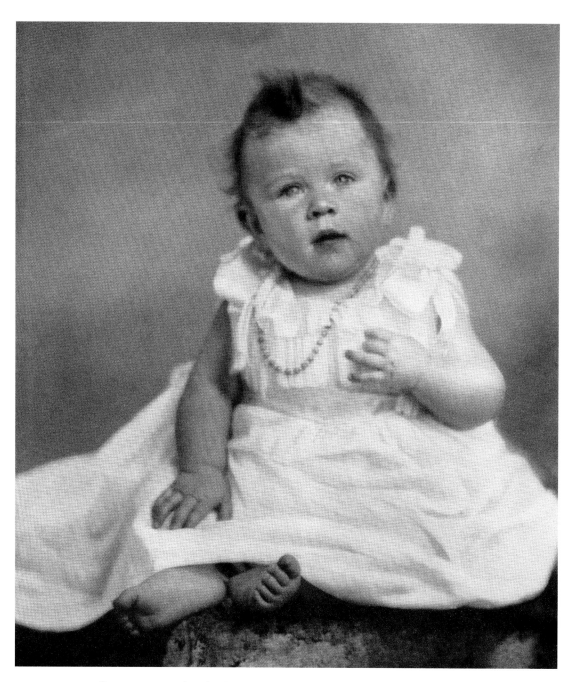

One newspaper referred to Princess Elizabeth as "the world's best-known baby".

Princess Elizabeth and Princess Margaret in 1932. The future Queen had about thirty toy horses.

Crawford came from Edinburgh to be the princesses' governess in 1933. She arrived to find the seven-year-old Elizabeth in bed, pretending to drive her horses, tying her dressing gown cords to the bedsteads. "I mostly go once or twice round the park before I sleep, you know," she said. Horse mad, the little girl had thirty or so toy horses. Every night they were fed and watered and lined up neatly outside the nursery. The girls began their day bouncing on their parents' bed. Elizabeth had lessons from 9.30am until 11am with Crawford. The rest of the day was passed in exercise, dancing, singing, a short rest and an hour in which "Crawfie" read to her. The princesses played with their mother before supper and enjoyed card games before bed. Queen Mary thought Elizabeth needed more history, but the Yorks preferred their daughters to be running about outside.

In 1936 everything changed. "It was plain to everyone that there was a sudden shadow over the house," Crawford wrote. Elizabeth's grandfather died within a year of his Silver Jubilee. At the end of the year Edward, Prince of Wales, abdicated to marry Wallis Simpson and Elizabeth's father, poor, unprepossessing Bertie, had to become George VI.

"I was overwhelmed," the new King said. Unlike his brother, however, he had a trump card in a perfect little family.

Elizabeth was destined now for quite a different future. She was heir to the throne. Elizabeth attended her father's coronation in 1937. She sat with Queen Mary and Margaret and took a keen interest in proceedings. "I thought it all very, very wonderful," she wrote in a little book she made for her parents.

The family had to leave their Piccadilly home for the cavernous and rather gloomy Buckingham Palace. Crawfie compared it to "camping in a museum" and Lilibet thought it so big that "people need bicycles". There were dozens of staff and police detectives on guard. The new King and Queen no longer had the time to play every day with their children, but the Queen tried to give her daughters a "normal" childhood, arranging the 1st Buckingham Palace Guide Company, with an attached set of Brownies for Margaret. Elizabeth and Margaret practised semaphore in the palace corridors and cooked sausages over fires in the gardens.

Queen Mary's enthusiasm for history finally won the day. In 1938 Elizabeth was sent to Eton twice a week to learn constitutional history from the Vice-Provost of the school, Henry Marten. As they ploughed through the constitutional scholarship of Sir William Anson, Marten told her that the British monarchy's strength was its adaptability, and he talked of the importance of broadcasting. As he saw it, speaking directly to the subjects via the radio encouraged their loyalty. It was a useful lesson for Elizabeth, who would go on to become an accomplished broadcaster.

The war changed everything for "us four".

The girls moved to Windsor, Elizabeth begging her father for a greater role. Her work with the Auxiliary Territorial Service (ATS) was vital to war propaganda – and throughout her life she has felt a special bond with war veterans. After the war the 19-year-old princess was flung once more into the public eye. Her days were taken up with correspondence and public engagements – opening factories, presenting prizes, addressing delegations and Girl Guides – as well as being Colonel of the Grenadier Guards.

The palace did, however, turn down the offer of an honorary degree from Cambridge University. It wouldn't do for the princess to seem too intellectual.

For her 21st birthday Elizabeth received a car from her parents with the numberplate HRHL. On the day itself she was in South Africa on tour. She gave a speech on the radio to the Empire and Commonwealth. As she said: "I can make my solemn act of dedication with a whole Empire listening." Her dedication was one of self-sacrifice and duty. People all over the world listened as she said: "I declare before you all that my whole life, whether it be long or short, shall be devoted to your service."

She was ready to be Queen.

Elizabeth, shown here in 1932, took ballet lessons after her studies.

The Queen's love of horses endured throughout her life.

King George VI and Queen Elizabeth with Princess Elizabeth and Princess Margaret in the grounds of Windsor Castle in 1936.

Princess Elizabeth with her mother and sister in 1940, the year following the outbreak of the Second World War.

The teenage princess studied constitutional history to prepare for her new destiny.

～ King Edward's Farewell ～

At 10 o'clock last night Sir John Reith announced on the wireless:–

"This is Windsor Castle. His Royal Highness Prince Edward."

The former King then broadcast the following message:–

At long last I am able to say a few words of my own. I have never wanted to withhold anything, but until now it has not been constitutionally possible for me to speak. A few hours ago I discharged my last duty as King and Emperor, and now that I have been succeeded by my brother, the Duke of York, my first words must be to declare my allegiance to him. This I do with all my heart. You all know the reasons which have impelled me to renounce the Throne. But I want you to understand that in making up my mind I did not forget the country or the Empire which as Prince of Wales, and lately as King, I have for 25 years tried to serve. But you must believe me when I tell you that I have found it impossible to carry the heavy burden of responsibility and to discharge my duties as King as I would wish to do without the help and support of the woman I love. And I want you to know that the decision I have made has been mine and mine alone. This was a thing I had to judge entirely for myself. The other person more nearly concerned has tried up to the last to persuade me to take a different course. I have made this, the most serious decision of my life, only upon the single thought of what would in the end be best for all. This decision has been made less difficult to me by the sure knowledge that my brother, with his long training in the public affairs of this country and with his fine qualities, will be able to take my place forthwith, without interruption or injury to the life and progress of the Empire.

And he has one matchless blessing, enjoyed by so many of you and not bestowed on me – a happy home with his wife and children.

The Times, December 12, 1936

As Prince of Wales, Edward VIII served in the Grenadier Guards during the First World War. He became King when his father, George V, died in 1936, but he abdicated in order to marry Wallis Simpson, an American divorcée.

A PRINCESS AT WAR

by Valentine Low

On the evening of September 3, 1939, King George VI broadcast to the nation: "For the second time in the lives of most of us, we are at war." Princess Elizabeth and Princess Margaret sat close to the wireless in Scotland, listening. Elizabeth was 13.

The princesses remained in Scotland until after Christmas, when they moved to Royal Lodge, then Windsor Castle. The King and Queen lived at Buckingham Palace and refused to listen to government pleas that they should escape to Canada or the United States. As the Queen said: "The children will not leave unless I do. I shall not leave until their father does, and the King will not leave the country under any circumstances whatsoever." In Windsor the children continued lessons, ate their rations in darkness and spent evenings in the air-raid shelter under the castle. They were ready to flee at any time and slept in "siren suits": all-in-ones beloved of Winston Churchill.

Prewar, suggestions that Elizabeth might broadcast on the radio were rebuffed. In 1940, the palace changed its mind. Elizabeth gave a speech during *Children's Hour* on the BBC to Britain and North America, aimed at evacuees. As she told them, she and Margaret "feel so much for you, as we know from experience what it means to be away from those we love most of all". It was a propaganda hit in America.

Elizabeth longed for a greater role in the war effort. The King refused. When she turned 16, Elizabeth graduated from the Girl Guides to the Sea Rangers (senior Guides had been known as Rangers since 1920). The Sea Rangers focused on naval training and Elizabeth gained her boating permit and practised dinghy sailing – and went on short camps where she joined in with the daily chores. In 1945 she was promoted to Sea Ranger Commodore.

Princess Margaret looks on as Princess Elizabeth broadcasts in 1940.

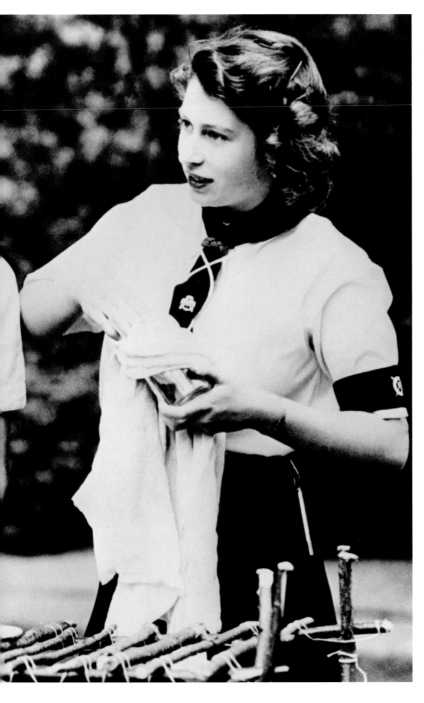

Elizabeth happily mucked in with her fellow Sea Rangers. She joined in 1943.

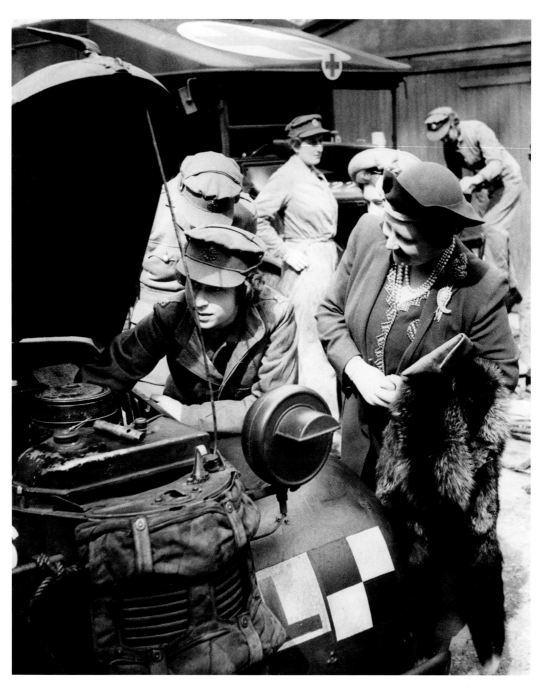

The princess during ATS training, under the watchful eye of her mother, Queen Elizabeth, in 1945.

Yet Elizabeth wanted to do more. She begged her father to let her join the services. "I ought to do as other girls of my age do," she said. Finally, the King allowed her to join the Auxiliary Territorial Service (ATS) in March of the same year. By this point women had adopted nearly all army driving work.

Elizabeth didn't sleep in the camp dorm in Aldershot. She returned to Windsor each night. However, she worked hard. She had never even held a spanner before, and so, as she said, "everything I learnt was brand new to me – all the oddities of the inside of the car and all the intricacies of map-reading". She later told the politician Barbara Castle that it had been the only time she had been able to test herself against people the same age as her. Photographs of her at work appeared on the cover of *Time* magazine and every Allied newspaper. She loved her work, and found driving thrilling.

On May 7, 1945, the BBC interrupted a piano recital to announce that the next day would be known as Victory in Europe Day. On May 8, the princesses appeared on the balcony of Buckingham Palace, Elizabeth wearing her ATS uniform. That night she and Margaret, with their governesses and some Guards officers, set off to celebrate, dashing incognito through the crowds. As Elizabeth remembered, "all of us were swept along by tides of happiness and relief".

Princess Elizabeth takes the wheel of an ATS ambulance in 1945.

Princess Elizabeth, Preparation for Future Responsibilities

Princess Elizabeth will be 18 years old next Friday. Notwithstanding a recent Act, correcting a constitutional anomaly, which has drawn special attention to the birthday, this is neither a coming-of-age nor a "coming out." But 18 is something of a landmark in any girl's life, whether she be princess or milkmaid; and especially in war-time, for it is the age of registration. Princess Elizabeth is no longer a child; she is already beginning to move more freely among her future subjects. Without any "building up" of an entrance, a new character has slipped demurely upon the stage of public life. She has few lines to speak at present, but in a later act she will have many. The audience will watch with a lively curiosity the gradual revelation of her character. She is, of course, like any young girl, very much the product of her upbringing. The lines, though clear, are lightly traced. It is for life to determine which of them shall be more deeply etched.

It has been the first care of their Majesties to secure to their daughters a natural and normal childhood; to prepare the heiress indeed for her future responsibilities, but to shield her from their premature impact. They have aimed at providing the sort of environment that the most enlightened English parents of their own generation would best like their children to grow up in: a comfortable and cultivated home, with an atmosphere of affection, easy manners, and reasonable discipline.

The real director of the Princess's education has been and is the Queen, its immediate supervisor a young Edinburgh graduate, Miss Crawford, who has upheld through the years of tutelage the standards of simple living and honest thinking that Scotland peculiarly respects. Specialist teachers have been called in to help; but the Princess has not been encouraged, nor has she desired, to become a specialist.

A sound physical education has provided the background of all her studies. She is a good horsewoman, and rather more than a good swimmer, and she enjoys all the outdoor sports and amusements natural to her age. War, which in some ways has been cramping for her, has in this respect been kind. She has had to share the common lot of her contemporaries in frequent separation from her parents; on the other hand, she has enjoyed a greater proportion of country life than might have fallen to her in peace. On the academic side the Princess's education has been mostly in modern subjects, and pursued on a wide front. Like some others of her sex, she is no mathematician. But she took kindly to modern languages, and speaks both French and German fluently and well. She has read many of the classics of French literature, and of course many more of English. If her literary education shows any bias it is towards history, as is proper to one called to her peculiar destiny…

Princess Elizabeth stands for the generation that will inherit the coming victory – she will live in a new world, and will be the representative of those who have to mould it. None may prophesy what the circumstances of their and her future will be; what is essential above all is the ability to master them, however unexpected the form they take. Freshness, simplicity, and the undiminished capacity to learn – all native qualities of youth – are the condition of achieving that mastery. These have been preserved in Princess Elizabeth partly by her education, but even more by her own innate sense of their supreme value.

The Times, April 17, 1944

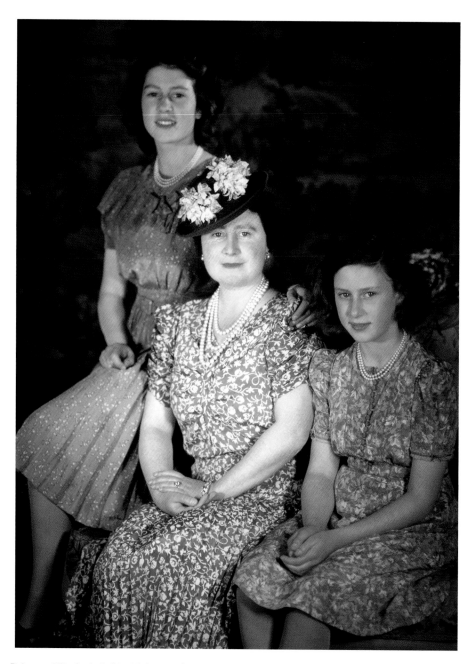

Princess Elizabeth (left) with her mother, Queen Elizabeth, and sister, Princess Margaret, in 1944.

Princess Elizabeth shortly after she turned 18, holding Susan the corgi.

Night Scenes in London, Royal Family on Palace Balcony, Rejoicing Crowds

The biggest crowd seen outside Buckingham Palace since the Silver Jubilee, outnumbering even those of the Coronation, greeted the King and Queen and the two Princesses when they appeared on the balcony last night. The people packed the pavements and the roadway in front of the Palace, and for a long way down The Mall. They stood in silence listening to the King's broadcast speech, and at the end of it raised a great cheer, and sang the National Anthem. Then the crowd began to chant: "We want the King." A few minutes later the King and Queen appeared on the balcony with the Princesses, and waved and smiled to the crowds. The King was in naval uniform, and the Queen was wearing a white ermine wrap over her evening gown and had a diamond tiara in her hair. For five minutes there was a tumult of cheering.

About 10.45 the King and Queen and the Princesses again came out on to the balcony, where they stayed about 10 minutes, waving to the crowd in response to cheers. Shortly before midnight, when searchlights were being flashed across the sky, their Majesties appeared on the balcony again, and remained there for a few minutes. When they returned to the palace most of the crowd left for home. Earlier the two Princesses, escorted by Guards officers, had left the palace to mingle with the crowd outside.

Everywhere crowds listened silently to the loud-speaker relays of the King's speech. Some 60,000 people in Trafalgar Square, bareheaded, joined in singing the National Anthem. A crowd of about 10,000 listened in Parliament Square. In Whitehall, as soon as the King had finished speaking, bandsmen of the Grenadier Guards played outside the Ministry of Health and the crowd sang and danced. There was also dancing in other parts of London.

Floodlighting drew great crowds to Buckingham Palace after dark.

St. Paul's Cathedral was also impressively floodlit, by A.T.S. girls. Trafalgar Square was flooded with light as Nelson's Column was illuminated, and the crowd grew to about 100,000 as streams of people converged on the square.

The Times, May 9, 1945

Crowds gather to see the royal family waving from the balcony of Buckingham Palace on VE Day.

*Princess Elizabeth,
with Queen
Elizabeth, King
George VI and
Princess Margaret
on the balcony of
Buckingham Palace
on VE Day, May 8,
1945.*

A PRINCESS
IN LOVE

"HOW HIGH HE CAN JUMP!"
by Kate Williams

"How high he can jump!" said Elizabeth to Marion Crawford, in July 1939. The princess and her governess were watching the handsome 18-year-old cadet Prince Philip of Greece leaping over nets on the tennis courts, while her parents made an official visit to the Royal Naval College in Dartmouth. It was 1939, just before the outbreak of the war. Elizabeth was 13 and had lived a sheltered life. Her second cousin once removed, clever, international Philip of Greece was a revelation.

Elizabeth was entranced, much to the delight of Philip's uncle Dickie Mountbatten, who had engineered the meeting. Philip was invited to join the family for tea on the royal yacht, moored near by – and Elizabeth watched, fascinated, as Philip ate a banana split. When the royal yacht departed Dartmouth, the cadets followed in their little boats, until the King commanded them to turn back. They obeyed – apart from Prince Philip, who rowed hard after them. Elizabeth watched him through her binoculars. Officials shouted at Philip through a megaphone until he finally turned – but the die had been cast. Philip found the young princess very appealing – cheerful and practical, she was unlike his fragile mother.

Philip was born in Corfu in 1921, the only son, and fifth and final child, of Prince Andrew of Greece and Denmark and Princess Alice of Battenberg. When Philip was one, a popular uprising forced his uncle King Constantine I of Greece to abdicate, and Prince Andrew was exiled from Greece. The family set up in Paris but disintegrated – his mother was put in an asylum and his father took a mistress. Philip was sent to boarding schools and flourished at Gordonstoun in Scotland before going to Dartmouth.

Princess Elizabeth (front, third from left), with King George VI, Lord Louis Mountbatten, known as Dickie to the family, (standing, third from right) and Queen Elizabeth (centre front) during the visit to the Royal Naval College, Dartmouth, 1939. It is thought that this is where Princess Elizabeth first met Prince Philip (standing, second from right).

Prince Philip was born in Corfu, Greece, in 1921. He is pictured here in his naval uniform.

*Elizabeth and Philip attend the wedding of Lady Patricia Mountbatten,
Philip's first cousin, in 1946 – the year before they became engaged.*

During the war, Philip wrote regularly to Elizabeth and came to stay for Christmas in 1943. With the end of hostilities, he came to court the 19-year-old future queen in earnest. Occasionally they went to concerts or restaurants; at other times they stayed in the nursery with Margaret and drank orangeade. Elizabeth's circle was not enthusiastic. The King and Queen wished her to "see more of the world" and "meet more men" before marrying. There was concern among courtiers that Philip was not quite the right sort – "no gentleman" – and he signed visitors' books as of "no fixed abode". Elizabeth refused to listen. She had been set on Philip since Dartmouth; the separation of war had only intensified the romance. The King had to relent. The engagement was announced on July 9, 1947, with the wedding fixed for November 20.

The government and courtiers worried that a lavish ceremony might infuriate a population deep in a postwar recession. However, Winston Churchill called it "a flash of colour on the hard road we have to travel" – and his view won. The marriage of the young princess and her handsome prince would be as magnificent as possible. Yet the day could not be a bank holiday; one day off might plunge the faltering economy into dire straits. Clothes rationing was still in force and thousands of women donated clothing coupons for the dress – but the Palace returned them, because coupons could not be transferred. The Privy Purse found the money for the silk and Norman Hartnell designed the dress, inspired by Botticelli's *Primavera*.

Three thousand presents poured in from all over the world – and half were put on display. Elizabeth received jewels, china, vases, a racehorse, a home cinema, more than 150 pairs of silk stockings, and 500 cans of tinned pineapple from the governor of Queensland. Perhaps the oddest was two pieces of toast, sent by two young women in London who had burnt it in excitement when they heard about the engagement on the wireless.

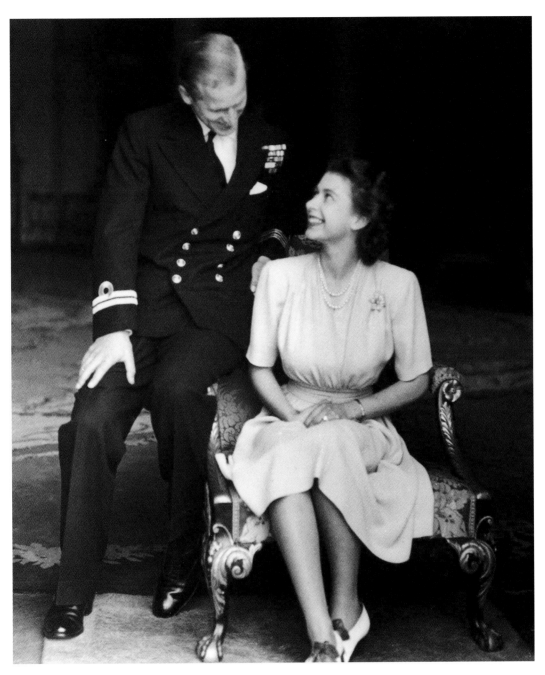

Princess Elizabeth and Prince Philip at Buckingham Palace on July 10, 1947, after their engagement was announced.

Two nights before the wedding, the King and Queen held a ball for the royal guests at Buckingham Palace. The King led a conga through the royal apartments. It was a true postwar jamboree. Among those not invited, however, were Philip's three surviving sisters, who were married to German princes. Also staying at home were the Duke and Duchess of Windsor. Neither the princess nor her mother could forgive him for abdicating.

"I can't believe it's really happening," Elizabeth said to her old governess on the morning. At Westminster Abbey, the King escorted his daughter up the aisle, followed by her two five-year-old pageboys, cousins Prince Michael of Kent and Prince William of Gloucester, Princess Margaret and seven other bridesmaids. About 2,000 people were crammed into the stalls – the choir had to sit in the organ loft with the radio commentators. Elizabeth made her vows and promised to obey her husband – which would be technically impossible when she became Queen.

After the ceremony, 150 guests travelled to Buckingham Palace to dine on partridge casserole (partridges were unrationed) and Bombe Glacée Princess Elizabeth. The cake was created by supplies sent by the Australian Girl Guides, and stood 9ft high and weighed 500lb. While guests dined, news footage was packed up and sent all over the world.

The couple left for their honeymoon first to Hampshire, then Birkhall on the Balmoral estate, through cheering crowds, despite the rain. At the palace, the royal family felt rather deflated. "I can't imagine life without her," said Margaret. Elizabeth had enjoyed the most wonderful day. "I was so happy and enjoying myself so much that I became completely selfish," she wrote to her mother. She hoped that from now on the government would see her as an adult rather than a child.

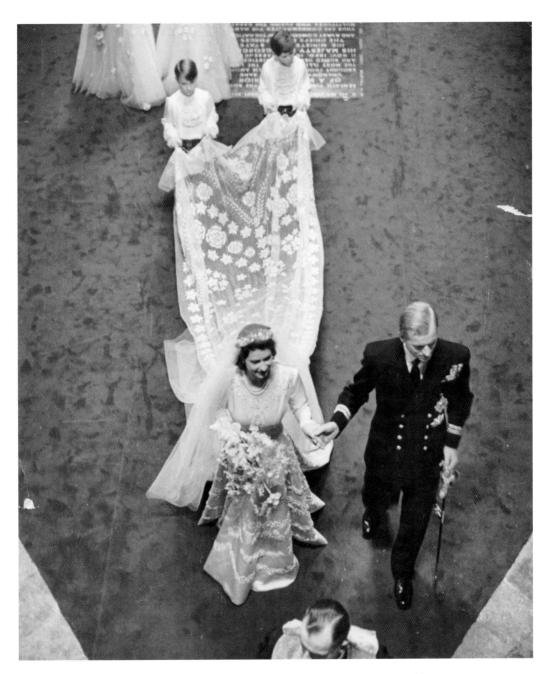

The newly married couple walk down the aisle of Westminster Abbey.

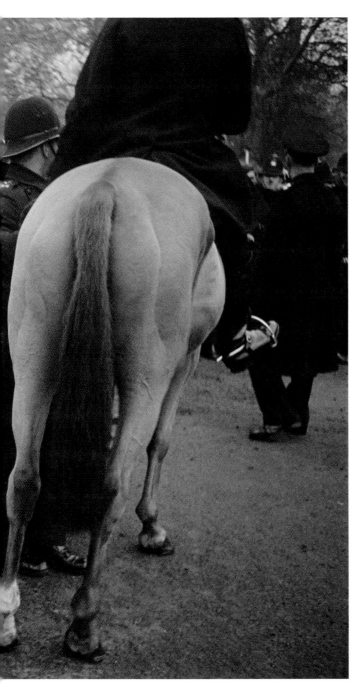

*Police hold back
crowds outside
Buckingham Palace
after the wedding.*

Marriage of Princess Elizabeth.
∽ The Ceremony in the Abbey. ∽

By a spontaneous gesture the whole company in the nave rose in their places to honour the entry of Mr. Churchill as he walked alone to his stall in the choir. At 11 o'clock the Precentor and two Minor Canons, vested in copes of stately gold and crimson, escorted to their places in the sanctuary the first procession of royal guests, including Lord and Lady Mountbatten and other near relatives of the bridegroom. A tumult of cheering outside the Abbey at 11.16 distracted the attention of the congregation from the arrival of the Duke of Edinburgh and his groomsman, Lord Milford Haven, who slipped in by way of Poets' Corner in the inconspicuous manner of the bridegroom's party at any ordinary wedding. This great ovation saluted the arrival of the Queen's procession, which now, meeting Queen Mary at the west door, moved with measured pace up the whole length of nave and sacrarium and

were conducted to chairs within the sanctuary. The mothers of bride and bridegroom walked together, until Princess Andrew left the Queen to go to the gospel side, with the bridegroom's other relatives; Queen Mary followed with the King of Norway. When the bride's family had taken their places the front row was occupied by the Queen, Queen Mary, both of these wearing the ribbon of the Garter, the Duke of Gloucester, in khaki, and the Duchess, the King of Norway, the Duchess of Kent, and the young Duke in a kilt of Royal Stuart tartan. Next to arrive was the procession of the visiting clergy, the two archbishops, with white and gold mitres and the crosses of Canterbury and York carried before them, and with them the Moderator of the General Assembly of the Church of Scotland. The prelates went to the sedilia on the south side of the altar. Meanwhile the collegium of the Abbey itself, not only the Dean and Chapter but the lay vicars, the choristers, and the King's scholars – that privileged body who represent the voice of the lieges in the acclamation of the crowned King – had gone down in procession to the west door to meet the bride. A fanfare of silver trumpets, sounded in King Henry V's chantry above the shrine, went pealing up to the ancient vault; and precisely at half past 11 the entire college bowed to their Sovereign and Visitor as he entered the Abbey Church with the bride upon his arm. According to the custom of royal brides the Princess wore her veil so that her face was not covered, and she looked at once happy and singularly childlike as she followed the great procession of clergy up the nave, directing a shy smile towards a group of former members of the Royal Household who were sitting on the right. But the expression in the eyes of the King was that of any father who is filled at once with pride in the daughter he is handing into another's care and with unfeigned delight in the happiness she has found. The clergy parted to left and right as they reached their stalls, and the bridegroom and groomsman emerged from their inconspicuous place to form a row of four with the King and the Princess at the top of the sanctuary steps. Behind the bride her two pages, Prince William of Gloucester and Prince Michael of Kent, in white shirts and tartan kilts, held her train clear of the lowest step, and behind them again the eight bridesmaids, all in white with white wreaths and bouquets, stood in the gangway under the lantern, in the middle of the space that at a coronation is called the theatre. As the procession advanced the choir had been singing the hymn "Praise, my soul, the King of Heaven"; with its last notes Princess Margaret stepped forward to take the flowers from her sister's hands, and the Dean, bowing to the King, began the marriage service.

For the signing of the register the bride and bridegroom passed behind the altar into the Confessor's Shrine, and the King and Queen, Princess Andrew, Princess Margaret, the Duke of Gloucester, the King of Norway, and Lord Milford Haven accompanied them. In their absence the choir sang that anthem of Samuel Wesley which sounds with such notes of victory, confidence and praise its many variations on the phrase "the word of the Lord endureth for ever". It ended, and the Kneller Hall trumpets pealed forth again from King Henry's Chantry, in a fanfare that seemed yet prouder and richer than that which had greeted the entrance of the bride. The banners of the Abbey were brought out into the sanctuary facing the doors of the shrine, whence the royal family emerged, led by the Queen, and returned to their places. Last of all came the bride and bridegroom, walking hand in hand, the bride's train carried for the moment by Princess Margaret. As they passed down the line they paused opposite to Queen Mary, and made reverence with curtsy and a deep bow. It was a charming epilogue to a ceremony full of beautiful associations; and then, still walking hand in hand, with joy in their eyes and pride and hope in their mien, they passed down through choir and nave and went out to meet the plaudits of the people.

The Times, November 21, 1947

Princess Elizabeth and Prince Philip wave to the crowds from the balcony of Buckingham Palace on their wedding day.

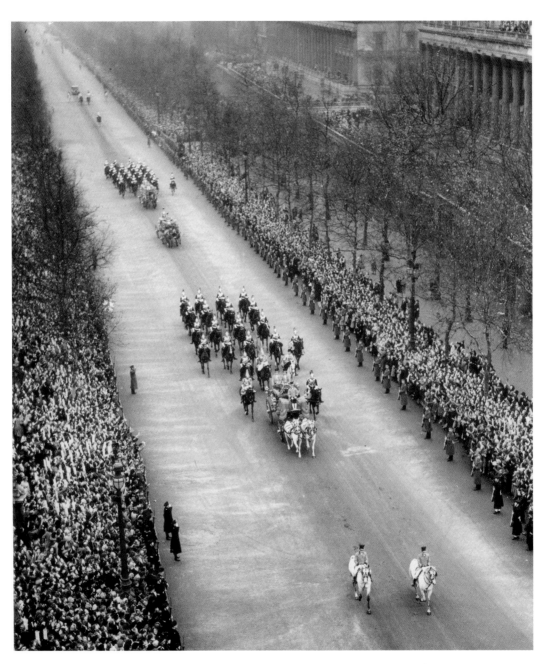

The royal wedding, November 20, 1947: Princess Elizabeth's coach and escort.

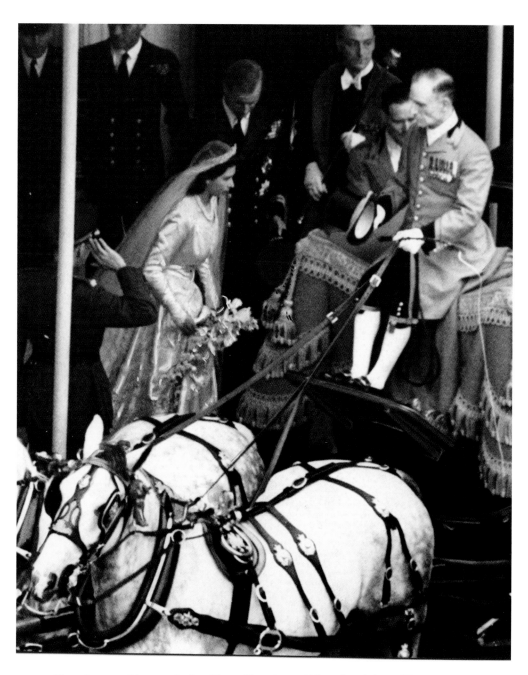

The princess and her new husband leave Westminster Abbey after their wedding ceremony.

The married couple.

HIS OWN MAN

by The Times & James Owen

Whatever the subsequent frustrations caused him by his role as Elizabeth's husband – and there were many – Philip would always remain true to himself. Indeed, it was this independence of mind, this certainty of self, this tireless masculinity, that had attracted her to him. These qualities also enabled him, more than was perhaps appreciated during his lifetime, to become the most successful of consorts.

Philip's character was forged during an upbringing that obliged him to become self-reliant at an unusually early age. A great-great-grandson of Queen Victoria, he was born into the house of Schleswig-Holstein-Sonderburg-Glücksburg, Danish aristocrats who had been placed on the Greek throne in 1863.

In 1922, a year after Philip's birth, a revolution stemming from Greece's defeats in Turkey led to the abdication of his uncle the King (whose own father had been assassinated in 1913). Soon after, the royal family was forced into exile, although the monarchy would be restored in 1935.

By then, however, Philip was following his own destiny. His parents had moved to Paris, but before Philip was ten his father, Prince Andrew, a soldier who had been blamed for Greece's military failings, had become estranged from his wife, Alice. In 1930 she was hospitalised for treatment of what was diagnosed as paranoid schizophrenia.

To shield him, Philip was sent to Britain, where he was looked after by his Mountbatten cousins, whose surname he adopted. After attending Cheam, a preparatory school in Surrey, he was educated at two rather unorthodox schools. The first, Schloss Salem near the Bavarian Alps, was an institution where liberality of mind was imparted in a rugged and austere physical environment.

*Prince Philip (centre) was born into the Greek royal family, but spent most of his life
as a pillar of the British royal family, as the Duke of Edinburgh.*

When the Nazis forced the school's Jewish founder, Kurt Hahn, to flee, he established a new school in a new country: Gordonstoun, near Inverness in Scotland. Philip followed, and thrived. Hahn's early appraisals of his pupil – "lively intelligence", "meticulous attention to detail and pride of workmanship", "capacity to derive great fun from small incidents" – continued to ring true. Unlike many of his class, Philip was also open-minded and curious about the world.

In 1939, at the age of 18, Philip entered the Royal Naval College at Dartmouth in Devon. He graduated top of his class, having received commendations including Best Cadet. His capability was apparent from the start and, had his life gone differently, he would undoubtedly have risen to the top of the service on his own merits.

During the war, Philip served on battleships and saw combat in different parts of the world. In the Mediterranean he was involved in the battle for Crete and saw action against the Italian fleet at Cape Matapan, where he was mentioned in dispatches for his conduct. In 1945 he witnessed the Japanese surrender at Tokyo Bay.

The man that Elizabeth decided to marry had much more experience of the world than she. Despite this, Philip knew that as a consort he would have to "fit into the institution" and avoid "getting at cross-purposes, usurping others' authority".

Even so, the progressive naval officer was determined to dispense with much of the flummery at court. When he and the Queen moved into Buckingham Palace, he noticed that a bottle of whisky was placed by the Queen's bed each night. It transpired that this had been a request of Queen Victoria's which had never been changed. Philip rescinded the custom. He also had dishwashers installed in the kitchens and put an end to the 18th-century practice of footmen wearing powdered wigs.

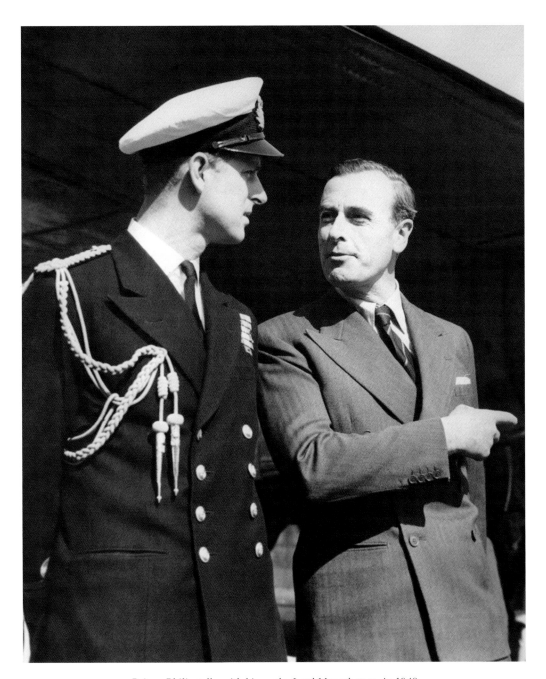

Prince Philip talks with his uncle, Lord Mountbatten, in 1948.

Philip's urge for change would often be thwarted by the conservatism of courtiers. Clashes were inevitable, not least with the Queen Mother, who at first refused to move out of Buckingham Palace, and these were aggravated by the duke's forthright, sometimes abrupt manner – the cause of the gaffes with which Philip later became associated in the public mind.

From the start Philip showed a fierce resolution to protect his wife from the increasing intrusion of the press and palace diary-managers. The greater the nuisance, the more his irritation would show. Nor did he ever have much time for politicians.

He retained his interest in science, engineering and technology – of which he would become a champion in the Fifties – as well as, perhaps more surprisingly, an interest in modern art. His most enduring achievement, however, conceived as early as 1956, was the Duke of Edinburgh's Award, and young people remained one of the prince's abiding concerns.

Philip's father had died in Monte Carlo in 1944, having not seen his son (or wife) for five years. As a father himself, Philip would come to expect a great deal of his children, and would sometimes be disappointed. Famously, he resented not being able to give his children his own (adopted) surname, claiming that he had so little input in such decisions that he was nothing more than an "amoeba". Moreover, his relationship with his eldest son, Charles, would not be easy – the two men had very different personalities.

In many ways, the duke and the Queen also led separate lives. They had their own dining rooms, sitting rooms and bathrooms, and the intimate side of Philip's life inevitably became a matter for speculation. His continued attraction to beautiful women after his marriage was certainly no secret, but his bond with his wife rested on deeper foundations.

Humour was a bedrock of their relationship, for he could always make her giggle. Reunited with the Queen at the end of her coronation, her husband eyed her crown and remarked: "Where did you get that hat?"

Prince Philip with his son, Prince Charles, in 1952. Philip and Charles later had a rather difficult relationship.

STRENGTH AND STAY

by Sally Bedell Smith

The indelible image of the Diamond Jubilee weekend in June 2012 was of the Queen and the Duke of Edinburgh standing on the upper deck of the royal barge for nearly four hours in the rain. Aged 86 and 90, enduring chill and blustery winds, they showed fortitude as well as gratitude to the 1.2 million people along the banks of the Thames.

It was everything that symbolised the royal couple. They were tough, stoic, duty-bound, a team. A beacon of continuity throughout decades of change, they set an example and solidified the traditions that help to bind the nation.

Their mutual devotion radiated a "sense of unqualified commitment that has been so characteristic of every aspect of this reign", said the Archbishop of Canterbury Rowan Williams when they celebrated their 60th wedding anniversary in 2007. Among the places they visited that year was Malta, where they had enjoyed a carefree existence as a young married couple when Philip was posted with the Royal Navy.

In 2015 they returned to the island nation for a state visit – a sentimental three days that took them back to favourite haunts such as the Marsa racecourse, where Princess Elizabeth had watched her husband play polo. On the first night they attended a reception for Malta's great and good. It had been a long day that included a three-hour flight and a welcoming ceremony, yet the Queen was animated and engaged as she circulated through the crowd, and Philip left a trail of laughter.

If the Queen was constant and calm, the Duke of Edinburgh was a spritz of vinegar with his irreverent and sometimes caustic comments. However, he always said "supporting the Queen" was his primary purpose as her consort and he held true to this for more than seven extraordinary decades. Her marriage to her "strength and stay" arguably held the royal family together through the divorces of three of their four children, and the harrowing week

The royal couple celebrate their silver wedding anniversary at Balmoral in 1972.

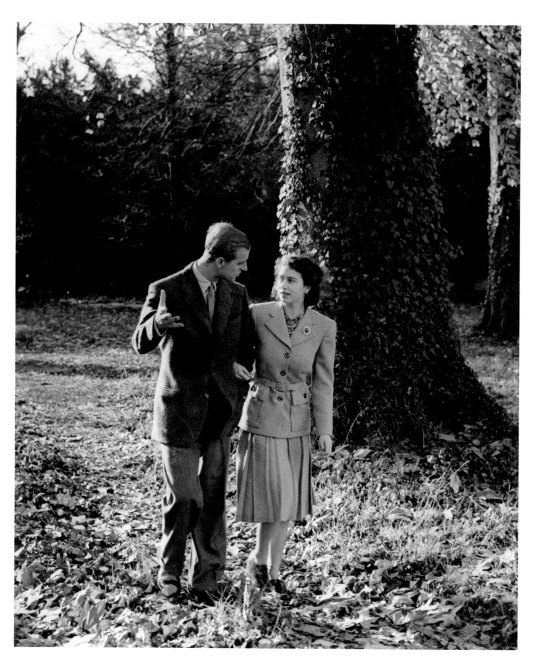

The princess and the duke pictured at Broadlands, Hampshire, in 1947, shortly after their wedding.

after the death of Diana, Princess of Wales. For Britain and the Commonwealth, their remarkable partnership created the most successful monarchy in history.

Princess Elizabeth could have chosen from what her friend Lady Glenconner called "a whole battalion of lively young men", English aristocrats with vast landholdings and wealth. Yet at the unlikely age of 13 she fell in love when she first spent an afternoon with 18-year-old Prince Philip of Greece. He was a naval officer in training and a distant cousin also descended from Queen Victoria and Prince Albert. He had very little money but he was strikingly handsome, confident, intelligent, breezy and energetic.

In the ensuing years Princess Elizabeth came to view Philip as a man of ideas and appealing complexity who would be neither easy nor boring but would share her commitment to duty and service. Despite a protective shell formed during a rootless childhood when he was neglected for long periods by his divorced parents, "Philip had a capacity for love which was waiting to be unlocked", said their mutual cousin Patricia Mountbatten.

Elizabeth "would not have been a difficult person to love", she added. "She was beautiful, amusing and gay. She was fun to take dancing or to the theatre." Her curly brown hair framed her porcelain complexion, with cheeks that the photographer Cecil Beaton described as "sugar-pink", vivid blue eyes, an ample mouth that widened into a dazzling smile, and an infectious laugh.

They were married on November 20, 1947, and spent their honeymoon at Birkhall, the 18th-century lodge on the Balmoral estate. "Philip is an angel," Princess Elizabeth wrote to her mother, "he is so kind and thoughtful." He in turn wrote to his mother-in-law: "My ambition is to weld the two of us into a new combined existence that will not only be able to withstand the shocks directed at us but will also have a positive existence for the good."

To a remarkable degree, that wish came true. They had only a few years together before she assumed the burdens of the crown at the tender age of 25. Their time in Malta from 1949 to 1951 was the closest Princess Elizabeth came to an ordinary existence – socialising with other officers' wives, going to the hair salon, even carrying her own cash, although shopkeepers noted "she was slow in handling money".

It was Philip who broke the news to his wife in 1952 that her father had died at the age of 56 and that she was now Queen. In the beginning Philip was viewed with suspicion by the old-style courtiers surrounding his wife. He was excluded from the substance of the Queen's official life, with no access to the state papers in her daily boxes. Yet he carved out a significant role for himself as a patron of more than 800 charities and advocate for causes from wildlife conservation to youth fitness, even as his wife came to rely on him for advice when making tough decisions.

If her advisers brought a question to her on a matter outside her head-of-state role, she asked them first to find out what Philip thought. Her approach to problems was to look at the big picture and ask for other options, while Philip drilled down and got to the heart of a problem – what one of her advisers called "a defence staff rigour", with an ability to "pull an idea to bits, find the good parts and the parts that need work". Her advisers knew that if her husband was happy with an idea, she probably would be as well. Early on, Philip saw the potential of television for the monarchy. He encouraged the Queen to use it and even tutored her on how to read from an autocue for her first televised speech in 1957.

On their trips around the United Kingdom and overseas, they perfected a choreography of turns and cues that appeared effortless. He would watch her intently during their walkabouts to see whether she needed any assistance. He would often spot people who couldn't see her – children in particular – and guide them out of the crowd to a better vantage point. When the Queen needed a boost, he was there with a humorous aside: "Don't look so sad, sausage."

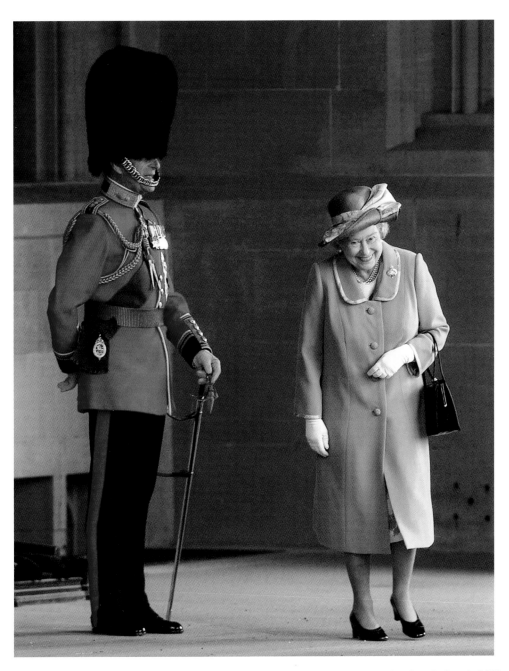

The Queen gets the giggles as she passes the Duke of Edinburgh in uniform at Buckingham Palace in 2005.

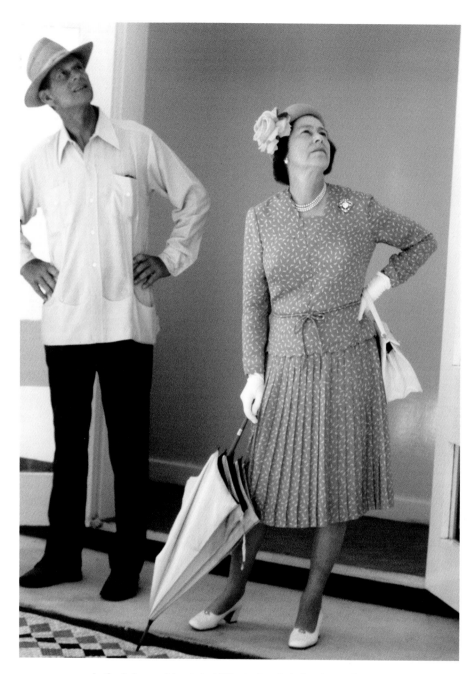

In the Solomon Islands in 1982, during their South Pacific tour.

*One of a series of portraits taken at Buckingham Palace in November 2001
to commemorate the Golden Jubilee the next year.*

On board a private jet – a scene from the 1969 BBC film Royal Family.

In a greenhouse at Balmoral, 1972.

Arriving at St Paul's Cathedral for a service of thanksgiving held in honour of the Queen's 80th birthday, June 15, 2006.

I VOW TO THEE, MY COUNTRY

LONG LIVE THE QUEEN
by Valentine Low

Because King George VI died in his sleep, of a coronary thrombosis, it is hard to put an exact time on the moment Princess Elizabeth became Queen. This much is certain, however: she was high up in a fig tree in Kenya, surrounded by wild animals, and did not hear the news until some hours later.

She and Philip were staying at Treetops, a game-viewing lodge in a tree overlooking a waterhole where they could watch the wildlife, on the first leg of a tour that was due to take them to Australia and New Zealand.

On the morning of February 6, 1952, knowing nothing of what had happened at home, they returned to Sagana Lodge, the farm given to them by the Kenyan government as a wedding present. Eventually Michael Parker, one of the royal party, was told the news over the phone by Martin Charteris, the Queen's private secretary, who was at a hotel a few miles away.

Parker crept around the house to attract Philip's attention and beckoned him out on to the lawn. The news left the prince utterly shocked. "He looked," Parker recalled, "as if you'd dropped half the world on him."

By the time Charteris found the new Queen, she was at her desk drafting letters of apology for the cancellation of the tour. "What are you going to call yourself?" he asked. "My own name, of course," she replied. "What else?"

On her way back to London she changed from the jeans she had been wearing at Sagana Lodge into the mourning clothes that always travelled with her. Outwardly she was calm, a woman who despite her relative youth – she was 25 – appeared ready for the role that fate had thrust upon her; inside, she was doing her best to conceal the grief she felt at the loss of her father.

On the tarmac at Heathrow, after a 24-hour journey, she was met by Winston Churchill. The prime minister – who was accompanied by the leader of the opposition Clement Attlee; the lord president of the council

Lord Woolton; and the foreign secretary Anthony Eden – seemed so overcome by emotion that he could not speak.

The next day, at St James's Palace, at her formal proclamation as Queen, Elizabeth spoke of "this heavy task that has been laid upon me so early in my life". She said: "My heart is too full for me to say more to you today than that I shall always work, as my father did throughout his reign, to uphold constitutional government and to advance the happiness and prosperity of my peoples, spread as they are all the world over."

It is a promise she kept for longer, and with a greater devotion to duty, than anyone might have imagined.

Upon hearing the news of the death of her father, the new Queen appeared outwardly calm.

~ Death of the King ~

It is with profound regret that we announce the death of the King at Sandringham early yesterday. The following statement was issued from Buckingham Palace. "It was announced from Sandringham at 10.45 a.m. today, February 6, 1952, that the King, who retired to rest last night in his usual health, passed peacefully away in his sleep early this morning." The Duke of Edinburgh broke the news to the new Queen in Kenya. After hurried preparations had been made, they flew from the little landing ground near Nyeri to Entebbe, Uganda, to join their airliner Atalanta. A tropical storm delayed their departure from Entebbe for two hours. They left just before midnight (8.47 p.m. G.M.T.) and are expected to reach London at 4.30 p.m. today. The Queen and Princess Margaret were at Sandringham when the King died. His Majesty had been out shooting on the previous day. The Accession Council, at a brief meeting at 5 p.m. yesterday, signed the Proclamation of Queen Elizabeth II.

This is described in the constitutional textbooks as a body which is something more than the Privy Council and one which represents "a more ancient assemblage, the Witan or Commune Concilium meeting to choose and proclaim" the new Sovereign. The large attendance at the Council included the Lord President, Lord Woolton, the Prime Minister, the Foreign Secretary, the Chancellor of the Exchequer, Mr. Attlee, Mr. Herbert Morrison, many other Ministers, Opposition front benchers and private members of Parliament who are Privy Councillors, Lord Mountbatten, representatives of several other countries of the Commonwealth, and the Lord Mayor and other representatives of the City of London. One of the Commonwealth Privy Councillors at St. James's Palace was Sir Arthur Fadden, Deputy Prime Minister of Australia. He heard of the King's death and the Council meeting while he was visiting Napoleon's tomb in Paris. He chartered a special aeroplane to London and arrived at the Palace just as the Council was dispersing. He was in time to add his name to the list of signatures on the Proclamation. An interesting feature of the text of the Proclamation is the designation of Queen Elizabeth as "Head of the Commonwealth". She is the first Sovereign who has been so proclaimed on accession to the Throne.

The news of her father's death was broken to the Queen by the Duke of Edinburgh at 2.45 p.m. local time (11.45 a.m. Greenwich time). It was first given to the Royal Lodge by a representative of the East African Standard, who was reporting the royal tour and received a news agency message from his office in Nairobi, and by Major Charteris, who both spoke from the same telephone box in the Outspan Hotel, Nyeri, 17 miles from the Royal Lodge, at 2.10 p.m. Lieutenant-Commander Parker informed the Duke, and they waited until official confirmation had been received at the Royal Lodge by radio-telephone. The Duke then broke the news to his wife. She was resting after spending the night at the Treetops Hotel, in Aberdare Forest, watching big game. Arrangements for their departure were hurriedly made and the royal couple left the Lodge at 5.30 and drove to the airfield at Nanyuki, which lies on the equator.

The Queen wore a beige dress, a white hat, and white shoes, and the Duke a grey lounge suit with a black tie. The streets of Nanyuki through which they passed were filled with silent crowds. The natives said *Shauri mbaya kabisa* – "the very worst has happened" – when they heard the news. It was nearly dark when the royal car reached Nanyuki, and flares had been placed round the edge of the airfield in case they should be needed, but it was desired to avoid lighting them if possible as the grass was so dry that fire was feared. The Queen looked as if under strain when she stepped from the car, but she acted with great courage and smiled graciously at everyone.

The Times, February 7, 1952

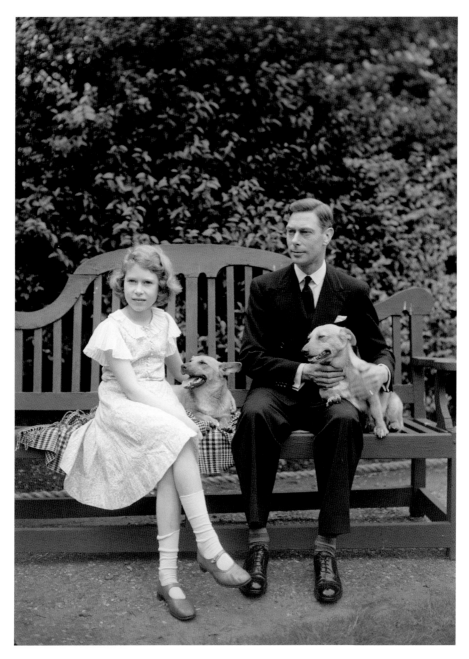

Princess Elizabeth and the Duke of York with their corgis in July 1936,
just a few months before the duke became King.

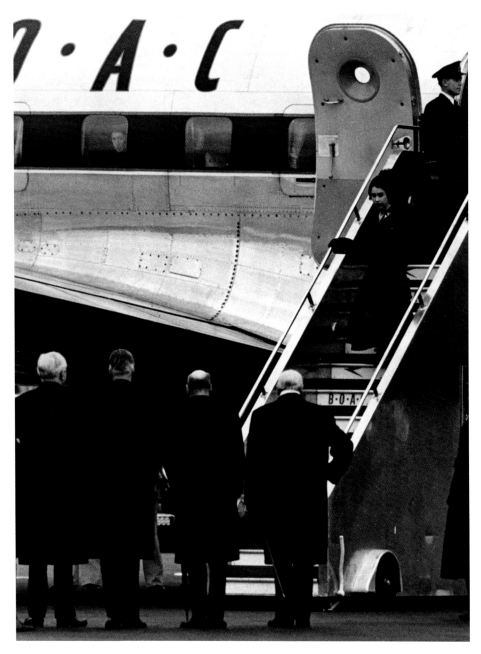

The new Queen is met at Heathrow on February 7, 1952, by (right to left) Winston Churchill, Clement Attlee, Anthony Eden and Lord Woolton.

THE LIGHT SHINES IN THE DARKNESS

by Ian Bradley

Although reserved about what she rightly regarded as a personal matter, the Queen made no secret of her Christian faith. Together with her belief that she was called and anointed by God, it sustained and strengthened her throughout her reign. There were very few Sundays when she was not in church, and her regular attendance was a matter of conviction rather than duty.

She was, of course, brought up in the Christian faith and schooled in the Victorian virtues of duty, discretion and dignity by her parents. There is some evidence that as a girl she felt that she was at the receiving end of rather too much religious teaching. At the age of ten she is said to have responded when asked by the Archbishop of Canterbury, Cosmo Gordon Lang, whether she would like to join him in a walk through the Sandringham gardens: "Yes, very much, but please don't tell me anything more about God. I know all about Him already."

The next year she wrote an account of her father's Coronation complaining that "at the end the service got rather boring as it was all prayers". These early protestations aside, Princess Elizabeth soon showed that she had the same strong faith as her father, grandfather and great-great-grandmother. In her first broadcast, made at the age of 14 during the darkest days of the war in October 1940, she spoke directly to children who had been evacuated from their homes, telling them: "God will care for us and give us victory and peace."

It was in her later Christmas Day broadcasts that she most clearly revealed the strength and nature of her faith. In the first five decades of her reign these were often essentially glorified travelogues. A radically new tone was introduced in the 2000 broadcast when the Queen, speaking directly to camera, made what could only be described as a personal testimony: "For me the teachings of Christ and my own personal accountability before God provide a framework in which I try to lead my life."

This particular broadcast attracted 25 times more letters to Buckingham Palace than any previous royal Christmas message.

Encouraged by its reception, the Queen continued to make frequent allusions to her faith in subsequent Christmas broadcasts. In 2002, reflecting on a year in which she mourned the deaths of her mother and sister and celebrated her Golden Jubilee, she said: "I know just how much I rely on my own faith to guide me through the good times and the bad." In her Christmas Day broadcast in 2015, she quoted from St John's Gospel – "The light shines in the darkness, and the darkness has not overcome it" – and spoke of her personal identification with this message.

Although rooted in Protestant Christianity, and feeling most at home with its tenets and style of worship, she reached out warmly and generously to those of other denominations and religious traditions. In her 2004 Christmas broadcast she movingly retold the parable of the Good Samaritan and called for greater understanding and respect between those of different faiths and cultures. This was a heartfelt and oft-repeated plea, springing from her belief in the power of religion as a force for good and reconciliation, and in the continuing validity of the teachings of the world's leading faiths.

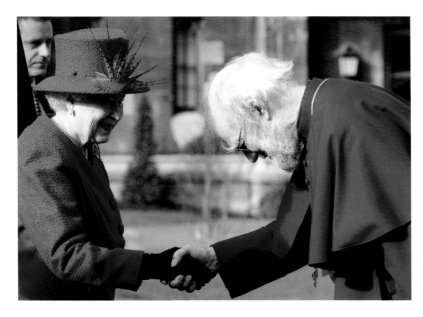

With the Archbishop of Canterbury, Rowan Williams, in 2012.

THE CORONATION

by Valentine Low

The Queen was only 25 when her father died, but for all the shock of his death she appeared to be as prepared for her new role as she ever would be. Two days later she was at St James's Palace for the Accession Council, where she made the Accession Declaration and took an oath to preserve the Church of Scotland. One of those present recalled how "a slight figure dressed in deep mourning entered the great room alone, and, with strong but perfectly controlled emotion, went through the exacting task the Constitution prescribed".

The other side of that dedication to duty was always a tendency to traditionalism, a reluctance to change things unless there was a good reason to do so. However, that did not mean that the Queen was ever a stick-in-the-mud, determined to adhere to the old ways at all costs. This was demonstrated early on in the volte-face made by the Palace over the question of whether television cameras would be allowed into Westminster Abbey for the Coronation.

During the planning the modernisers were keen to have the ceremony televised, while the traditionalists were opposed, arguing that it was essential to preserve the mystique of royalty. It was also felt that there were moments of the ceremony that were so sacred they should remain private. The Queen sided with the traditionalists, as did Winston Churchill, who felt that allowing in television would put too much strain on the Queen, and an announcement was duly made that television cameras would be banned from the abbey.

There was immediate uproar. The papers demanded, "Let the people see the Queen", and the Palace soon beat a hasty retreat. It was the Queen herself, who had originally thought that the cameras would be inappropriate, who decided it was time to listen to the people. As Sarah Bradford wrote in her biography: "When she saw how much her people wanted to see her actually crowned and how outraged they were that they should be excluded from a spectacle confined only to high officials, peers and foreigners, Elizabeth became convinced that the ban was a mistake." The television cameras were allowed into the abbey, but – in a last concession to those wanting to preserve at least some of the magic – they were not allowed to film the anointing and the communion, the most sacred parts of the service.

For everyone involved, the Coronation was heavy with the weight of symbolism. For the government, still wrestling with postwar austerity, the new Queen represented the nation's fragile hope. It was also an opportunity to promote the cause of the newly established Commonwealth, one that the Queen adopted with equal enthusiasm. When Norman Hartnell was designing her coronation dress, she asked him to embroider it with the symbols of the Commonwealth countries, such as the lotus flower of Ceylon and the wattle of Australia, as well as the traditional British emblems of the English rose, the Scottish thistle and the Welsh leek.

Above all, though, it was a solemn and sacred statement of her pledge to serve her people. After taking the Coronation Oath, in which she promised to govern her peoples – in Britain and overseas – according to their respective laws and customs, and to maintain the "Protestant reformed religion established by law", she moved to the altar and, laying a hand on the Bible, swore: "The things which I have here before promised, I will perform and keep. So help me God."

The Queen kissed the Bible and signed the oath, and then took her place in St Edward's Chair, where, under a canopy held unsteadily by four Garter knights, the Archbishop of Canterbury anointed her, saying: "As Solomon was anointed by Zadok the priest and Nathan the prophet, so be thou anointed, blessed and consecrated Queen over the peoples whom the Lord thy God hath given thee to rule and govern."

*The Queen, in the Gold State Coach, passes cheering crowds
en route to Westminster Abbey for her coronation.*

*Queen Elizabeth II and the Duke of Edinburgh wave at the crowds from the Buckingham Palace
balcony after Elizabeth's coronation on June 2, 1953.*

During Queen Elizabeth II's coronation at Westminster Abbey.

The seriousness with which the Queen regarded the promises she made that day is the key to how she governed her life thereafter. The fact that she regarded her position not as an honour, or a privilege, or even a calling, but as a sacred duty meant that she never shrank from her commitment to serve. It could be seen in the attitude she took to her work. She read the content of her red boxes without fail, from the latest cabinet minutes to the weekly summaries from her realms across the world. Whether it was the latest Foreign Office correspondence or a briefing from Canada in French (no translation required; the Queen was fluent in French), all are studied and carefully digested. She kept her weekly meetings with the prime minister right up until the very end of her reign.

"She is very assiduous and careful about reading things and when you discussed things with her, she had read them very carefully," her former deputy private secretary Mary Francis once said. "You don't very often get a question or a comment. But you know it's all sinking in and almost certainly some of it gets played back when she meets the prime minister at her weekly meeting or has her audiences with new ambassadors."

Harold Macmillan, her prime minister at the beginning of the 1960s, wrote in his diary that he was "astonished" at her grasp of detail. The Queen's dedication to duty was so much part of the fabric of the nation, an aspect of her which people came to expect without question, that it was still taken for granted even when she reached her nineties.

Well into her ninth decade the Queen carried out a solid 400 engagements or so every year. On one notable occasion in 2014, at the end of a state visit to France that included an official ceremony in Normandy to mark the 70th anniversary of the D-Day landings, the Queen undertook a morning of engagements in Paris, only to dash back to Britain by helicopter in time for the Epsom Derby.

In 2015, the year that Elizabeth became the longest reigning monarch in British history, she undertook 341 engagements – 306 in the UK and 35 abroad. Every day she the scanned newspapers and reviewed her correspondence – 200 to 300 letters a day.

Whether it was conducting the state opening of parliament, hosting foreign heads of state, or laying the wreath at the Cenotaph on Remembrance Sunday, the Queen showed at 90 an energy and a resilience that would be remarkable in a woman 20 years younger.

The Covid-19 pandemic necessarily curtailed this programme, even as she finally began to entrust more of her burden to the younger generations of the royal family.

The newly crowned Queen on the balcony of Buckingham Palace, as Prince Charles, Princess Anne, Prince Philip, the Queen Mother and Princess Margaret look on.

The Queen Crowned at Westminster

From the moment when the great procession – as majestic as its name – made its infinitely slow progress from the west door to the Sanctuary until the last ceremonial act had been fulfilled television held it all within its compass – or nearly all. The great mystery of the Anointing was veiled from sight beneath the silken canopy and the greater solemnity of the reception of the Blessed Sacrament by the Queen and her Consort was a moment too sacred for intrusion. But millions saw the culmination of the tremendous drama when St. Edward's Crown was uplifted in a majestic gesture by the Archbishop of Canterbury and descended gently in all the flashing splendour of sovereignty on the youthful brow, bowed to receive it. The stillness and composure of that slight, graceful figure, lustrous in the stiff habiliments of monarchy, endowed the moment with an enormous sense of historic import.

The hush was soon to be engulfed in acclaim, but the effect was unforgettable. Prince Charles was there to see it, in the protective presence of his royal grandmother. A few moments later his father came to perform that humble, tender act of homage, to swear as liege man of life and limb and to salute with a kiss his Queen and his wife. It was as husband and consort, also, that he knelt beside her in one of the most moving episodes of the great ceremony to receive a special blessing from the Archbishop.

Nothing was more memorable in the long solemnities than the manner in which her Majesty bore her part in them. Not only at the Crowning but in every movement and gesture there was a deep sense of recollection. Dignity went hand in hand with modesty, simplicity with majesty, gravity with a charm which shone like crystal within all that glitter of imperial and ecclesiastical effulgence.

When the last ceremony was completed to its perfect and shapely end, and the last echo of the great Te Deum had died, when the slow recession had withdrawn its splendid tide of pomp and colour from the shining Sanctuary, the multitudes outside prepared to receive their Queen. They had shared wholeheartedly in the singing of the "Old Hundredth", which by a nice touch of imaginative forethought had joined the nation in the vocal offering of the service. And now was the moment of acclaim for their newly anointed and crowned Sovereign. To those who had borne her on her way to the Abbey with thunderous cheers were added thousands more who thronged the ribboned miles of the long return procession.

The capital had drawn to its heart a great concourse which left to a sabbath calm nearly every street outside the processional way. Rain beat heavily on the stalwarts who had braved the rigours of the waiting hours and it was still pouring from leaden skies when the first royal processions left the Abbey. But when the state coach began to move off in the wake of the endless ranks of service men and women already in position far along the route the sun struggled through its veils. Colour leapt into splendour, and metal shone like silver.

Silvery also rang the Abbey bells, mingling with the great cheer which thundered round the Queen. Framed in the golden elaboration of the coach she bowed her diademed head tirelessly, her smile as gay and brilliant as the sun. The dignity of sovereignty was lightened and gladdened now with the affection which responded to that which she drew to her. All along that coloured river of the processional way, from stands and pavements and windows, from trees and housetops the happy tumult swept her to her palace.

The rain came again before the coach had carried her and her consort to their home, but nothing dimmed the loyal fervour of her welcome.

When the gates of the Palace were closed and the troops of her realm, her dominions, and colonies had passed on their proud way out of sight the crowds swept in a great surge towards the Palace. A great cheer swelled to the sky – it could have been heard a mile away – when the Queen, in her crown, with the Duke and their two children, came from the tall windows on to the balcony to see the R.A.F. fly-past.

As the aircraft swept and thundered overhead the Queen and her consort waved repeatedly to the waving and cheering crowd. On the balcony they were joined by Queen Elizabeth the Queen Mother, Princess Margaret, the Duke and Duchess of Gloucester, the Princess Royal, the Duchess of Kent with her children, and Princess Alice, Countess of Athlone. The Duke of Cornwall and his sister joined enthusiastically in the salutation to the crowd. The royal appearance on the balcony lasted for 10 minutes, the focus of a great and sustained outburst of loyalty, which continued long after the royal group had withdrawn.

The Times, June 3, 1953

Queen Elizabeth II during her coronation, holding the symbols of monarchy – the orb and sceptre.

HEAD
OF STATE

HER MAJESTY'S GOVERNMENTS

by Valentine Low

Despite the entertaining fantasy promulgated by Peter Morgan in his play *The Audience*, no one really knew what was discussed during the weekly meetings between the Queen and the prime minister. Plenty of people asked, however. In the early days of her reign, when the Queen was in her twenties and Winston Churchill was more than half a century her senior, his private secretary Jock Colville noticed that as the two of them got to know each other, the meetings got longer and longer. "What do you talk about?" he asked the prime minister. "Oh, mostly racing," he replied.

For all Churchill's jocularity, it would be a mistake to suppose that the meetings were all gossip and small talk. She read her boxes and made sure she always knew what was going on. "The Queen," Edward Heath wrote, "is undoubtedly one of the best-informed people in the world."

The Queen still saw Boris Johnson – who had not been born when her fifth prime minister, Harold Wilson, came to power – once a week, the Covid-19 pandemic permitting. Inevitably, over the years the Queen had better relations with some of her prime ministers than others. One suspects, for example, that her relationship with David Cameron was not improved by his embarrassing indiscretion in revealing how she "purred" down the phone after hearing the result of the Scottish independence referendum.

Churchill adored her and always occupied a special place in her affections; the historian Ben Pimlott in his biography of the Queen described how the weekly meetings would take on an almost jaunty air. "The premier would arrive wearing a frock coat and top hat, with a gleam in his eye, and disappear happily into secret conclave."

Harold Macmillan treated their relationship as what Pimlott called a kind of "chivalrous fantasy", and she got on surprisingly well with Wilson (according to him), despite having little in common with him. He treated her as an equal and aides noted that their audiences grew longer over time. Wilson once described the meetings as the only times when he could have a serious conversation that would not be leaked, with somebody who wasn't after his job.

Not all of the relationships were quite so easy. When Heath first met her, he said: "I lost my nerve and said to her, 'Have you been busy lately, Ma'am?' 'That,' she replied, 'is the sort of question lord mayors ask when I visit cities.'" It did not get much better after that. Heath had no small talk and little time for women, and as a member of the household observed, "the Queen found Heath hard going".

Politically too they were at odds: she was a fervent believer in the Commonwealth, while Heath was a passionate European to the exclusion of all else and did not think much of the Commonwealth. In 1971 he wanted her to stay away from the first Commonwealth leaders conference in Singapore because of the expected furious reaction to his plan to resume arms sales to South Africa; it took an intense meeting between monarch and prime minister at Balmoral for her to agree.

Even the most confident and socially adept of prime ministers could be put in their place. Recalling his first audience, Tony Blair said: "She was ... direct. 'You are my tenth prime minister. The first was Winston. That was before you were born.' I got a sense of my relative seniority, or lack of it."

The lack of warmth between the Queen and Margaret Thatcher has been well-documented, if a little exaggerated. Over time, the Queen grew to respect Thatcher, who was a devoted monarchist; as one of her ministers observed, "no one would curtsy lower than Margaret".

While there may not have been animosity between the two women, there was a lack of mutual understanding. One story has it that the Queen said of her prime minister, in fond mock despair: "Mrs Thatcher never listens to a word I say." Thatcher, in turn, found some of the royal ways baffling, such as the Queen's habit of washing up after Balmoral barbecues with her bare hands. Famously, after one visit she sent her a pair of washing-up gloves.

In 1986, against a background of Thatcher riling some members of the Commonwealth by refusing to back sanctions against South Africa, *The Sunday Times* published a story saying that the Queen was dismayed by some of Thatcher's policies. This went beyond the Commonwealth crisis over South Africa, the paper said: "The Queen considers the prime minister's approach to be uncaring, confrontational and divisive."

The extent to which the Queen believed that was an issue that was long argued over and not satisfactorily resolved. It was, however, an impression that did not go away, although the biographer Hugo Vickers has argued that he knows for certain that the Queen was deeply upset by the way Thatcher was ousted in 1990 and immediately gave her the Order of Merit. Whatever their differences, there was always a respect between the women. When the Queen attended Thatcher's 80th birthday party as guest of honour, others were touched by the sight of the Queen taking Thatcher's hand as she raised her from a deep curtsy before guiding the frail former prime minister through the throng of assembled friends and admirers.

After Thatcher's death in 2013, the Queen broke with tradition to attend her funeral, the first time since the death of Churchill in 1965 that she had attended the funeral of a former prime minister. That, however, had been a state occasion; this was a personal choice, and one that Thatcher's family said would have left her "humbled".

As the Queen grew older, and her prime ministers younger, their relationship changed. When John Major – the first prime minister who was younger than the Queen – succeeded Thatcher, the Queen "discovered in him a more relaxed, congenial visitor than his predecessor", according to Pimlott.

Of the Queen's relationship with Gordon Brown, almost nothing is known. However, he did provide one of the more amusing prime ministerial moments of her reign when he appeared to get lost at a state banquet at Windsor Castle after walking the wrong way round the banqueting table. "Has the prime minister got lost?" the Queen asked. "He disappeared the wrong way at the crucial moment."

David Cameron, whose brother used to go to tea at Windsor because he was at prep school with Prince Edward, revealed how she would occasionally tease him. Although she never saw *The Audience*, she got wind of the scene in which she supposedly dozed off as Cameron bored her with the latest political machinations from Europe. Later, the (real) Queen told him that she had never fallen asleep during their weekly meetings. After a dramatic pause, she added: "Yet!"

Brexit inevitably dominated the short premiership of Theresa May, but whatever their respective personal views on the outcome of the referendum, the two women are said to have established a good rapport. With Liz Truss, it transpired, there was no time to do so.

While it is certain that the Queen did not show the slightest inclination to interfere in politics, she found it hard to avoid on a number of occasions. During the Suez crisis of 1956 the Queen was in the invidious position of being kept thoroughly informed, thanks to a stream of Foreign Office papers and telegrams, so much so that she knew more of what was happening than a number of ministers, some of whom were notoriously kept in the dark. It also put her in a dilemma with regard to the Commonwealth: did she tell Commonwealth leaders what she had been told in confidence, or did she betray their trust by withholding information that was relevant to their interests?

As for the Queen's position on Anthony Eden's Suez intervention, it seems she was not entirely neutral. "I think the Queen believed Eden was mad," recalled one palace aide. While she may not have gone so far as to protest against the Suez operation, one courtier recalled: "She may have said to Eden something like, 'Are you sure you are being wise?'"

Overseas visits produced their share of dilemmas. In 1961 the Queen had been due to visit Ghana, where the newly independent country was starting to move towards single-party rule and dictatorship. With violence and anti-British feeling on the increase there were valid arguments for cancelling the visit, balanced by fears that to do so would drive Ghana into the arms of the Soviet Union. "She is grateful for concerns about her safety," Macmillan recorded in his diary, "but impatient of the attitude to treat her as a woman."

Determined to support the Commonwealth, the Queen went, and she danced at a state ball with the Ghanaian president. In South Africa a nationalist newspaper complained of "the honoured head of the once mighty British Empire dancing with black natives of pagan Africa"; the Ghanaian press hailed her as "the greatest Socialist Monarch in the world".

One of the most controversial episodes in the Queen's political life came during the resignation of Macmillan as prime minister in 1963. He had been thinking – and dithering – about stepping down for some time, and then was forced into action when he had to go into hospital for a prostate operation. This was before the days when the Conservative party elected its leaders; the new leader was supposed to emerge through soundings, although there was no agreed mechanism as to how the process should work.

The ever-devious Macmillan, meanwhile, despite still recovering from his operation, was determined to mastermind the changeover from his hospital bed. Chaos ensued, with the leading contenders jockeying for position, the cabinet divided, backbench MPs throwing in their two ha'p'orth, and Macmillan doing everything in his power to ensure that the obvious candidate – Rab Butler, the deputy prime minister – did not get the job.

Buckingham Palace did its best to stay out of the fray, which served only to prompt speculation about what the Queen would do. In the event, Macmillan managed to organise it so that within three quarters of an hour of his eventual resignation the Queen was at his hospital bedside for a farewell meeting. She asked him for his advice, he suggested that she call for Lord Home (who would relinquish his title to become Sir Alec Douglas-Home), and she agreed.

According to Pimlott, the advice was thoroughly unconstitutional, although it may have been what she wanted to hear. An aide told him: "When she got the advice to call Alec she thought, 'Thank God'. She loved Alec – he was an old friend. They talked about dogs and shooting together. They were both Scottish landowners, the same sort of people, like old school friends."

It was, in Pimlott's view, "the biggest political misjudgment of her reign", although other constitutional experts, such as Vernon Bogdanor, disagree. In *The Monarchy and the Constitution* he says she correctly took the most straightforward course and avoided getting involved in the internal politics of the Conservative party.

The controversy caused by the selection process led to a change in the rules of the Tory party. Thus, by the time the Queen faced another constitutionally tricky moment – the 2010 general election, which was widely expected not to produce a party with an overall majority – her private secretary had done a thorough job of laying the groundwork with the cabinet secretary to ensure that when it came to the post-election horse-trading to choose a prime minister, a clearly defined process had been set in place. She was not going to get caught out again.

Dedication was the Queen's watchword. In hindsight, nothing could be more fitting than that her last public act should be to invite her 15th and last prime minister, Liz Truss, to form a government. She relinquished forever the responsibilities of her own, which she had so dutifully fulfilled for so long, just two days later.

*The two women didn't always see eye to eye, but no one would curtsy to the Queen
lower than Margaret Thatcher, who was a devoted monarchist.*

John Major was the first prime minister who was younger than the Queen.
She found him "more relaxed" than Thatcher.

The Queen with Gordon Brown.

The Queen is said to believe that Anthony Eden, left, was "mad" for intervening in the Suez crisis and asked him: "Are you sure you are being wise?"

Fellow Scottish landowner Sir Alec Douglas-Home, pictured with his wife, Elizabeth, would talk about dogs and shooting with the monarch.

The Queen told Tony Blair, her tenth prime minister: "The first was Winston. That was before you were born."

Harold Wilson said his audiences with the Queen were his only chance of a serious conversation that would not be leaked.

The Queen had a special bond with Winston Churchill, pictured here with his predecessor, Clement Attlee, and Attlee's wife, Violet.

The Queen is said to have teased David Cameron, here with his wife, Samantha, and the Duke of Edinburgh, that she hadn't fallen asleep in their meetings – yet.

THE QUIET DIPLOMAT
by Valentine Low

The Queen fulfilled her international role in a way that no British sovereign did before her. From her first triumphant tour as Princess Elizabeth to the delicate diplomacy of the 2015 Chinese state visit, she met many world leaders, and they were often highly impressed.

She worked a unique brand of magic. When the Chinese president Xi Jinping visited Britain in 2015, the palace welcome was treated by China as the sort of affirmation they could get nowhere else in the world. It was the same in Germany that summer when Angela Merkel abandoned a meeting on the Greek economy to spend more time with her guest. And the Queen was perhaps one of the few people capable of making Donald (and Melania) Trump seem happy to share the limelight.

Even though she was among the most stellar players on the international stage, the Queen showed a quiet magnetism that remained undiminished – to say nothing of a capacity to surprise. When she and Michelle Obama put their arms around each other at a Buckingham Palace reception, it showed the Queen to be warmer and more affectionate than some supposed, and less bound by protocol than those who surround her. The bond forged between them paved the way for a successful state visit by President Obama two years later.

Some bonds were stronger than others. When Vladimir Putin visited in 2000, he had tea with the Queen at Windsor Castle – a relatively brief visit that did not, presumably, feature any hugs. Three years later the Russian president paid a state visit that was notable, among other things, for his being 15 minutes late for the ceremonial welcome.

One of her warmest relationships was with Nelson Mandela. The South African president is reported to have been one of the few people who got away with calling her Elizabeth; she called him Nelson. They got off to a good start long before he was elected president. Recently released from prison, Mandela had been invited to the 1991 Commonwealth summit in Harare but, because he was not a head of government, he had not been invited to the Queen's banquet. Her courtiers, unsure what to do, asked her. "Let's have him," she said. They got on, it was said, "like a house on fire".

Mandela even got the Queen to behave in unQueen-like ways. On his state visit to Britain in 1996 he asked for a concert at the Royal Albert Hall instead of a banquet. When, during the rousing finale, he got up to dance, she did likewise. "Good heavens," said one establishment figure. "The Queen is dancing!"

The Queen with Nelson Mandela, president of South Africa, in 1996. The two had a strong friendship and he is said to have been one of the few to be on first-name terms with the monarch.

The Queen with Vladimir Putin at Windsor Castle, 2000.

The Queen with the German chancellor Angela Merkel, 2009.

The Queen with President Barack Obama, 2011.

In an era when we are accustomed to the international celebrity status of the Duchess of Cambridge, as she was, and before her Diana, Princess of Wales, it is easy to forget that the young Elizabeth had a star quality at least as great, if not greater. Crowds came out in their thousands to see her, and statesmen found themselves falling for her charms. In a postwar world short of glamour and fun there was fanciful talk of the "Faerie Princess". Later, when youth and beauty were no longer the most important weapons in her armoury, she employed her wisdom and experience to useful effect. On more than one occasion the British government owed some of its foreign policy successes to the backstage diplomacy carried out unnoticed by the Queen.

She won her first international admirers before she became Queen. As Princess Elizabeth, she undertook a tour of Canada in 1951 that included a trip to the USA. President Truman was smitten. Afterwards the British ambassador, Sir Oliver Franks, wrote to the King to say that when Truman appeared with her in public he conveyed "the impression of a very proud uncle presenting his favourite niece to his friends". Truman himself said: "When I was a little boy, I read about a fairy princess, and there she is."

His successor, Dwight Eisenhower, became a firm friend. When the Eisenhowers were guests at Balmoral in 1959 he admired some home-made drop scones and she promised to send him the recipe. Later, she wrote to the president: "Seeing a picture of you in today's newspaper standing in front of a barbecue grilling quail reminded me that I had never sent you the recipe of the drop scones which I promised you at Balmoral. I now hasten to do so and I do hope you will find them successful." She concluded: "I think the mixture needs a great deal of beating while making and shouldn't stand around too long before cooking."

Even the Russians were won over. When Nikita Khrushchev visited Britain in 1956 the Communist party general secretary likened her to "the sort of young woman you'd be likely to meet walking along Gorky Street on a balmy summer afternoon".

When Britain was negotiating to enter what was then called the Common Market, it tried to overcome French objections by inviting General Charles de Gaulle for a state visit in 1960 to charm him into submission. He was given a ceremonial welcome and a state dinner and was delighted that all the royal family came to a banquet at the French embassy. He appreciated the Queen's fluency in French and realised, he wrote, that "she was well-informed about everything, that her judgments, on people and events, were as clear-cut as they were thoughtful, that no one was more preoccupied by the cares and problems of our storm-tossed age". Unfortunately, de Gaulle still said "Non".

During her state visit to Morocco in 1980, after erratic behaviour from King Hassan II, including his failure to appear for a luncheon until 5pm, he pointed at Robert Fellowes, her assistant private secretary at the time, and said he was responsible for the "terrible muddle". The Queen rebuked him: "I'll thank you not to speak to my staff like that."

The Queen had to put up with some fairly unsavoury guests. She was uncomfortable entertaining Nicolae Ceaușescu, the Romanian leader, during his state visit in 1978; out walking her dogs in the gardens at Buckingham Palace, she hid behind a bush rather than converse with the dictator and his wife. She was most angry with President Mobutu of Zaire, who visited in 1973; his wife smuggled a small dog through customs and ordered it steak from the palace kitchens. The deputy master of the household was told: "Get that dog out of my house!" It was duly put on a plane to Brussels.

The Queen's one great advantage over most democratically elected leaders, and certainly all British statesmen, was that she had been around much longer than any of them. Her longevity proved useful in the Commonwealth crisis of 1979, when African leaders turned against Britain for what they saw as its failure to act against white-ruled Rhodesia.

The Queen with the Indian prime minister Indira Gandhi, 1983.

The Queen with Zimbabwe's president Robert Mugabe, 1994.

The Queen with President Bill Clinton, along with the First Lady Hillary Clinton and daughter Chelsea, 2000.

The Queen with US Secretary of State Hillary Clinton and the French president Nicolas Sarkozy, 2009.

The Queen with President Richard Nixon, Princess Anne and Prince Charles.

The Queen with the Polish president Lech Wałęsa, 1991.

The Queen with the Irish president Michael D. Higgins, 2014.

As the former Commonwealth secretary-general Sir Sonny Ramphal said: "Julius Nyerere [of Tanzania] and Kenneth Kaunda [of Zambia] and people like that from Africa were young men when she became Queen, making their way in political life. She knew them as young prime ministers and young presidents and so over many years they were friends."

The Commonwealth Head of Government Meeting in Lusaka, which Margaret Thatcher initially refused to attend, seemed set to be a disaster. "Britain was looked on with the greatest possible distrust," said a minister. Not the Queen, however; when she arrived the government-owned *Zambia Daily Mail* contrasted her "extraordinary loving heart" with Thatcher's lack of sympathy.

Sir William Heseltine, the Queen's deputy private secretary at the time, said that the Queen helped the foreign secretary, Lord Carrington, to win over Thatcher to his plan to persuade the conference that the Rhodesia question was best solved by Britain, not the Commonwealth.

As head of the Commonwealth, the Queen was seen as transcending national boundaries. Kaunda recalled a conversation in Lusaka: "She said, 'My friend, you and I should be careful. We are under the scrutiny of the British prime minister.' I looked up and Mrs Thatcher had her eyes fixed on us." Softened up by the Queen, Kaunda swept Thatcher on to the dancefloor after the opening banquet and the meeting ended with an agreement that led to the negotiations for the peaceful establishment of an independent Zimbabwe.

The Queen was brought into play during the Falklands crisis in 1982. Britain had American support for a military response to the invasion but it was important to strengthen the bond. During a stay at Windsor Castle Ronald Reagan found the Queen "charming, down-to-earth", and went riding with her. In a speech to parliament, he confirmed his backing for the UK over the Falklands.

In her eighties and nineties the Queen still played an important role. The success of her state visit to the Republic of Ireland in 2011, when she laid a wreath to fallen Irish nationalists, was a triumph of her brand of quiet diplomacy. In 2014 it was followed by a state visit by the Irish president, Michael D. Higgins, during which she shook hands with Martin McGuinness at Windsor Castle.

The important work was, perhaps, done behind the scenes. However, for many it is those moments in Dublin and Windsor that will go down in history – and the way the Queen, as always, played her role to perfection.

Guests listen to a speech by the Queen in honour of the president of Ireland,
Michael D. Higgins, at a state banquet in Windsor, April 8, 2014.

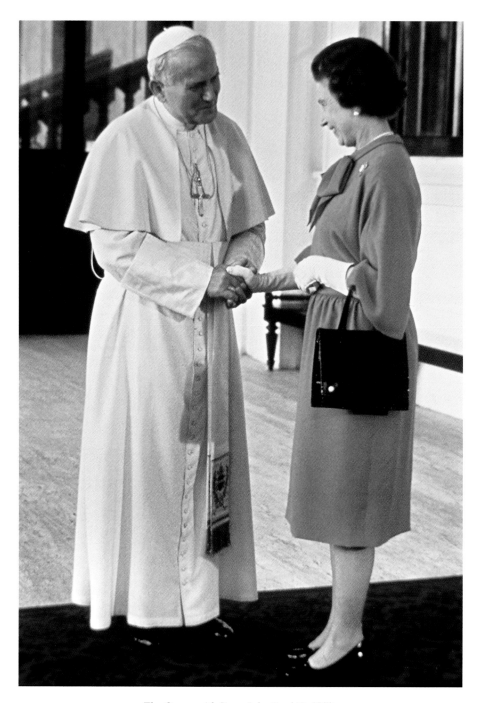

The Queen with Pope John Paul II, 1982.

The Queen with President Gerald Ford, 1976.

The Queen with Emperor Hirohito of Japan, 1975.

The Queen with President George W. Bush, 2007.

The Queen with Emperor Haile Selassie of Ethiopia, 1954.

The Queen making a toast at a state dinner in San Francisco, in 1983, with US president Ronald Reagan. The two got on famously, with Reagan calling her "charming" and "down-to-earth".

56 COUNTRIES, 92 LANGUAGES: THE COMMONWEALTH

by Giles Whittell

At most of the Queen's public events, her subjects turned out in her honour. At several, however, it was the Queen who did the honouring, and each time the object of her respect was the same – the Commonwealth.

No other institution except the monarchy itself bore the stamp of the Queen's personality as clearly as this sprawling collection of mainly English-speaking former colonies. It is not universally admired but in a sense it was her life's work. Its expansion was her proudest accomplishment on the world stage, and it is no coincidence that most of its 56 member states were represented at her various birthday celebrations.

The Queen's role as head of the Commonwealth gave the lie to the notion that she was powerless. As leader of a vast group of nations with shared aspirations, she wielded impressive power whether she liked it or not.

The Queen used this power most memorably in 2013 when, for only the second time in her reign, she did not attend the biennial Commonwealth Heads of Government Meeting (CHOGM). The meeting took place in Colombo. The Sri Lankan capital was recovering from civil war and its government was under condemnation for the deaths of about 100,000 civilian Tamils.

Aides said the Queen's non-appearance was not political. What did not need saying was that she was not going to fly halfway round the world to tarnish the Commonwealth by shaking hands with an alleged mass murderer. The effect for President Rajapaksa of Sri Lanka was devastating. In her place the Queen sent her son, and Prince Charles, in his main speech, avoided all mention of the civil war. He ended with a plaintive appeal to the "family values" that the Commonwealth represented. It was an awkward moment. Charles spoke for himself and his mother, and the subset of Commonwealth countries that successfully espouse democracy.

Overlooked in the fuss was the extraordinary fact that the Commonwealth exists at all; that it has expanded to include not just former British imperial possessions, but parts of Francophone Africa and a former Portuguese colony; and that it is the only international body apart from the United Nations to straddle the rich-poor divide on a global scale. The Commonwealth is loose enough not to break apart when stresses build, but coherent enough to function. It represents two and a half billion people – more than a quarter of the world's population. It promotes democratic ideals even if not all its members practise them.

The Queen was committed to the notion of a global English-speaking body from when she was a young woman. Her first tour of the Commonwealth as Queen started five months after her Coronation, covered 40,000 miles and lasted seven months. For her Silver Jubilee she went farther: 56,000 miles. At 76, she marked her Golden Jubilee with trips to Canada, Australia, New Zealand and Jamaica. With very few exceptions she attended Commonwealth summits not as an observer but as an exceptionally diligent chairwoman. She made a point of getting to know other leaders, the better to anticipate their moves and moods. She gave hundreds of gifts and accepted hundreds more, among them a totem pole and a canoe.

Her father, George VI, had not taken the idea of a durable successor to the empire seriously. As Richard Bourne, the former head of the Commonwealth Human Rights Initiative, puts it, running the Commonwealth "just wasn't as much fun as being emperor of India". The King's daughter was more concerned with duty than fun and understood that the Commonwealth had to be on the right side of history.

She had grave misgivings about Anthony Eden's bellicose response to the Suez crisis in 1956 and, according to her assistant private secretary at the time, may have gone as far as to remonstrate with him over his decision to retake the canal by force. She smoothed the path to Zimbabwe's independence, persuading Zambia's president Kenneth Kaunda to remove a potentially inflammatory reference to Robert Mugabe and Joshua Nkomo as "freedom fighters" from his speech at the Lusaka CHOGM in 1979.

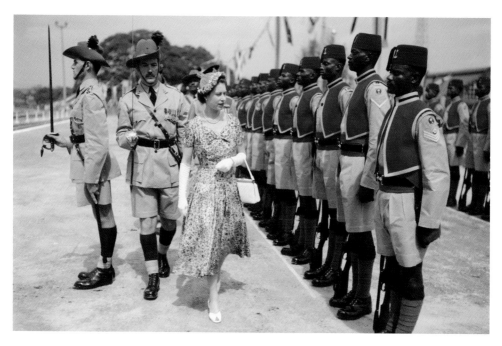

Inspecting the troops of the Queen's Own Nigeria Regiment, Royal West African Frontier Force, which had been renamed in her honour before her visit in February 1956.

The Queen is greeted by children dressed in carnival costumes in Port of Spain, Trinidad, in 2009.

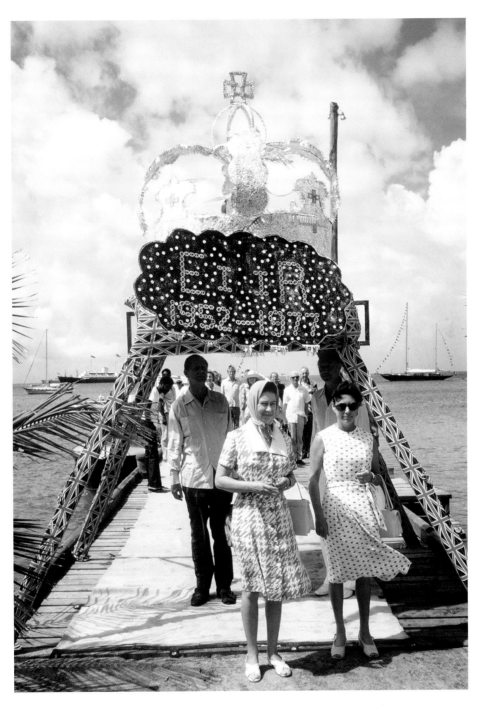

Princess Margaret, who had a house on Mustique, welcomes the Queen
to the Caribbean island during her Silver Jubilee tour, 1977.

The Queen and Prince Philip are entertained by Fijian traditional dancers on board the Royal Yacht Britannia, *1977.*

Visiting a wildlife park in Brisbane during her hugely successful tour of Australia, 2011.

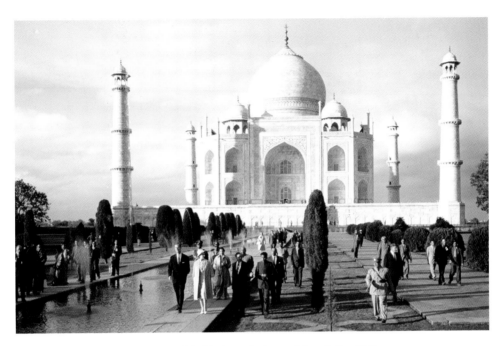

At the Taj Mahal in Agra during a visit to India, 1961.

The Queen in India in 1961, admiring the fashions.

She lobbied behind the scenes for democracy and against military dictatorship in Nigeria, and where democracy took root, she did her best to help it flourish. In one case highlighted by historians she was able to prevail on Ghana's charismatic president Jerry Rawlings to stand down at the end of his term (in 2001) rather than follow the disastrous example of some of Africa's self-appointed presidents-for-life.

Most importantly and courageously, the Queen sided with justice and the Commonwealth against Britain's own Conservatives in the long struggle against South African apartheid. It seems unconscionable now that Edward Heath defended selling arms to South Africa on the grounds that they would not be used to enforce apartheid and Britain had an inalienable right to set its own trade policies. The Queen thought it unconscionable in 1971.

She consented with reluctance to Heath's demand that she should not attend that year's CHOGM in Singapore. The government tried to persuade her not to go to the next meeting either, in Canada, but she went anyway.

The rift between Buckingham Palace and Margaret Thatcher over South African sanctions was deep and enduring. Thatcher's refusal to back the embargo led to a broad boycott of the 1986 Commonwealth Games in a personal humiliation for the Queen. She continued to attend summits even so, including an especially difficult one in Limassol in 1993 when Greek Cypriots branded her a killer for Britain's hanging of nine anti-British rebels nearly four decades earlier.

By the early 1990s the Commonwealth was limping. It had split over South Africa, played no role in ending the Cold War and was sidelined by the Queen's own government as an annoying irrelevance for having the temerity to lecture Britain on its moral shortcomings when its members harboured plenty of their own.

Yet it survived. More than that, it thrived. Over the next 20 years South Africa rejoined after a 33-year suspension, and non-Anglophone developing countries started to apply for membership. For Cameroon and Mozambique it was granted in 1995; for Rwanda in 2009; and in 2020 the Maldives became its 54th member. Gabon and Togo joined in 2022.

A 2011 report by the preposterously named Eminent Persons Group said the Commonwealth was drifting from its reformist mission and was hypocritical over human rights. Undaunted, the Queen urged it to dust itself down, respond to new challenges such as food insecurity and climate change, and "stay fit and fresh for tomorrow".

The same year, the Commonwealth had a long moment in the sun on the Queen's triumphant 11-day tour of Australia that took in Canberra, Brisbane and Melbourne. She opened that year's CHOGM in Perth, observing that such meetings' importance "has always been in precise relationship to their relevance". It was a neat, disarming touch. The theme of the summit was "women as agents of change" and she urged all to continue to strive together to promote the theme in a lasting way.

The Queen had been met at the start of the tour by Australia's first female prime minister. Julia Gillard, an avowed republican, had refused to curtsy and bowed awkwardly on the red carpet instead. Aides said the Queen "couldn't give two hoots". She swept all before her on her 16th visit to a country that has always reciprocated her affection. Before departing, she and Prince Philip were guests at a barbecue on Perth's Esplanade, attended by about 200,000 people.

Four years later, aged 89, the Queen resumed her role of leading the Commonwealth from the front. After the Colombo hiatus she took Prince Philip with her to host the heads of government in Malta. The trip was partly down memory lane, to a villa she had lived in before ascending the throne, but it was also the fulfilment of a duty to the Commonwealth she still cherished after more than 60 years.

The Commonwealth remains a popular and useful global forum – popular for the 5,054 athletes who competed in the 2022 Commonwealth Games, held in Birmingham, in England; useful for advocates such as Malala Yousafzai, shot in the head while going to school in Pakistan. The guest of honour at the 2014 Commonwealth Day service in London, Malala embodies the Commonwealth's ideals as well as the Queen herself.

Kenneth Kaunda, who was born in what was Northern Rhodesia in 1924, and who lived until 2021, once remarked that the transition from empire to Commonwealth was made possible by the Queen's personality. "Without that," he said, "many of us would have left."

The Queen with Kenneth Kaunda, 1979.

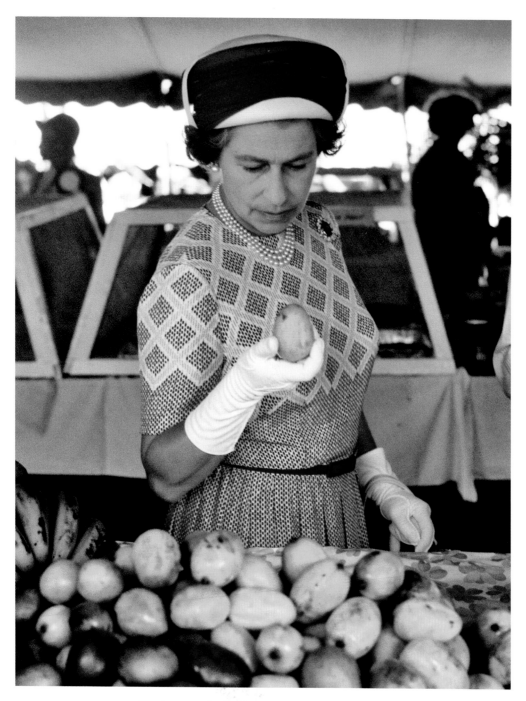

Touring a market in the British Virgin Islands, 1977.

QUEEN
AND COUNTRY

THE CROWN

by James Owen

Few Britons can remember when the Queen was not a part of their lives. Her life and reign were so long that the impact of their span will touch centuries yet to come, even as they were tinged by centuries past. The first prime minister to guide her, Winston Churchill, had been known in the late 19th century to her great-great-grandmother, Queen Victoria. The Queen's great-grandson, Prince George, whose time as sovereign will in some measure be shaped by her experiences, may still be king well into the 22nd century – nearly 80 years from now.

She grew up when the First World War was a recent memory. As a young woman, she lived through the Second World War, and as Queen she saw all the great events that have shaped modern Britain, from the Beatles to Brexit. The early years of the NHS, the end of austerity (the first time around), the Cambridge spies and the Profumo scandal, the Troubles in Northern Ireland, the Falklands War, the Iraq War, joining (and leaving) Europe, terrorist atrocities, "test tube babies", even a World Cup triumph at Wembley – she was there for all of it.

Motorways arrived, shillings went and the death penalty was abolished. A boy she saw playing a rabbit in a school play, David Cameron, grew up to become her 12th prime minister (before leaving to spend more time in his shepherd's hut).

She celebrated her first quarter of a century on the throne long before anybody began to carry around their own computers, let alone ones that made telephone calls. Her reign was long enough for her to watch it dramatised as history in the TV series *The Crown*.

Above all, she saw Britain's conception of itself change beyond recognition. The still substantial empire that she inherited went its own way, and the events of the Suez crisis in 1956 ended the pretence that the country was still a great world power.

Gone, too, is much of the class deference that underpinned the monarchy's role as the pinnacle of society. With these changes came more scrutiny and different expectations, altering steadily but fundamentally the Queen's relationship with her subjects.

In truth, the nature of the monarchy had already assumed a radically new shape following the event which made her heir to the throne. Amid its personal drama, what the abdication of her uncle, Edward VIII, really signalled was that whoever was sovereign had to accept that they could not do as they pleased. Their task was to keep the country united, not to cause division. Duty trumped desire, even happiness – a lesson that the young Elizabeth took to heart.

By the time of her Coronation in 1953, the belief that hers had to be a participatory monarchy was confirmed by the decision, reluctantly taken under pressure from public opinion, to televise the ceremony. Nevertheless, the Queen vetoed filming of the sacred moments when she was anointed and crowned.

Almost of equal significance, however, was the moment a few hours later when the press spotted Princess Margaret tenderly picking fluff from the jacket of Peter Townsend, the royal equerry with whom she was secretly in love.

The furore that ensued, as the Palace and the public grappled (as in 1936) with the consequences of a member of the royal family marrying someone who was divorced, marked the start of a new approach by the media to the Queen and her relations, focusing on their behaviour as individuals. It was a change in emphasis to which the Queen was slow to adapt.

Not a natural seeker of the spotlight – unlike Margaret – the Queen was instinctively conservative and particularly during the first part of her reign she heeded the advice of courtiers who shared her caution. This "safety first" approach meant that she rarely erred. Despite the social changes and conflict that Britain witnessed in 70 years, hardly ever, for example, did she express an opinion about politics that might have stirred up resentment.

Only once, according to her former private secretary Martin Charteris, did she feel that she had put a foot wrong. In October 1966, a spoil tip from a Welsh colliery, loosened by weight of rainwater, slid down onto the village of Aberfan below. The disaster claimed 144 lives, of whom 116 were children, most buried under the avalanche of mud that engulfed the local junior school. Many of their parents were miners who ran from the coalface to dig for survivors, largely in vain.

Although Prince Philip went to the site soon after, it was not until eight days later that the Queen herself visited it. Advisers had suggested that she go before but she had felt that her presence might detract attention from the rescue efforts. Her assistant press secretary at the time, William Heseltine, later said that in hindsight she thought that she ought to have gone there earlier. "It was a sort of lesson to us," he observed, "that you need to show sympathy and to be there on the spot, which I think people craved from her." Aberfan was one of the few occasions on which the Queen showed emotion in public, trying to hold back tears.

The documentary *Royal Family*, which aired in 1969, went further still in penetrating the façade. Commentators at the time fretted that it "let daylight in", removing any mystique that still clung to the Queen. Its revelation, however, that in private she and her children led lives not so different from many middle-class families began to reduce what appearance of distance from them there remained.

Yet what in the long run the public seemed to want was a fuller appreciation by the monarchy of what that distance should signify. The Queen was famous from when she was born. Anne Frank kept pictures of the "little princesses" on the walls of her wartime hiding place in Amsterdam.

The Queen and Prince Philip visiting Aberfan, October 29, 1966.

When she became Princess of Wales in 1981, Lady Diana Spencer was less used to that status, and less schooled in how it should be worn. Although she undoubtedly revelled in the attention that she drew, what people responded to was someone who looked royal but also openly empathised with the struggles of others. Nearer to a modern celebrity than a traditional royal, Diana had star power yet did not feel out of reach.

That impression was perhaps reinforced by the very public airing of her travails, with the Palace's muted response seeming old-fashioned by comparison. Another lesson had to be learnt in the aftermath of Diana's death in 1997, when the Queen's own wish was to remain at Balmoral to allow Prince William and Prince Harry to grieve in private.

Yet the mood in the country turned from shock at Diana's death to dismay as the Palace's lack of official response to it appeared chilly and unfeeling. For perhaps the only time in her reign, the Queen's hand, as the historian Hugo Vickers put it, was forced. She felt obliged to return to London to see the thousands of floral tributes left by the public for Diana and to make a live television address acknowledging the feelings of those who had laid them.

She described Diana as "an exceptional and gifted human being", and told the nation that she was speaking to them not just as their Queen but "as a grandmother" (a humanising touch added to her draft by Alastair Campbell, a journalist before he became adviser to the prime minister, Tony Blair).

In the 70 years since her Coronation, the two institutions central to the ceremony, and at the time to the British way of life, have had to renegotiate in an unprecedented fashion their relationship with those over whom they once held sway. The Church of England has undoubtedly struggled to find ways of remaining such a relevant presence in people's lives.

The Crown, perhaps more easily able to adapt its raison d'être, has succeeded better, especially in the two decades after Diana's death. Notable triumphs include the steep rise in public affection for the Duchess of Cornwall, once reviled as the "other woman" in Prince Charles's marriage, and one of his sons marrying a divorced, mixed-race woman, Meghan Markle.

Much of the credit for the affection in which the monarchy is still widely held was due to the Queen's resilience – a word that means not only tough but flexible. One only has to look to the royal houses of Spain or Belgium, among others, to see failures of judgement by her contemporaries that have gravely damaged their standing. The challenges that Charles and his heirs face will be different from those she met, yet if the House of Windsor is to continue to thrive, they too will have to move with the times.

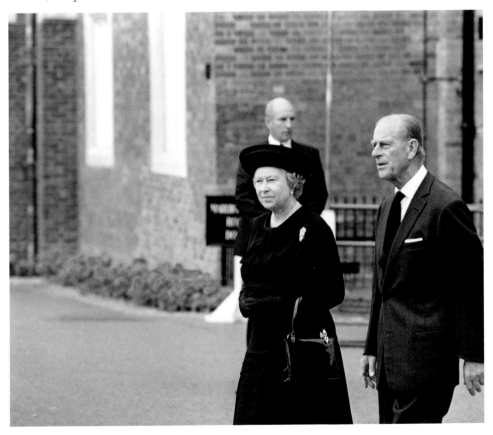

The Queen and Prince Philip arrive at the Chapel Royal to pay their respects to Diana, Princess of Wales, September 5, 1997, the day before her funeral.

Peace Returns to Aberfan, Villagers Moved by Queen's Visit

Aberfan is quiet. The great black tip that crushed Pantglas school is no longer the scene of feverish activity. With only a few workers of one contracting firm at the site, there is little to tell the tale of the past nine days.

There are still scores of police, but the faces have changed; uniforms are clean and bright and there is no weariness in their eyes. The villagers are getting used to the many strangers.

I spoke to some villagers today. Two things, they say, will never be forgotten – the terror of October 21 and the "kindness and sympathy" of the Queen who visited them yesterday.

The visit, as Mr. T. Griffiths, Chief Constable of Merthyr Tydfil, said on Friday, was to the people of Aberfan. "There will be no glory or royal glamour to this visit", he said. He was right. No cheers or flag waving welcomed the Queen and Duke of Edinburgh. The loudest noise was the sober choruses of "goodbye."

A young woman Red Cross worker told me today that it had been an almost painful sight. "The Queen seemed so near tears but she kept fighting them back. We all felt very close to her", she said.

While the royal couple were always surrounded by quiet villagers as they walked through the streets of Aberfan there was no pushing or jostling. The Queen stopped often to talk to those bereaved.

Councillor J. Williams and his wife Beatrice, who lost seven relatives in the disaster, were host to the visitors for 20 minutes. Tea was served in the front room of the Williams's home and the tragedy was explained.

The Queen appeared most moved as she accepted a small posy of flowers from Karen Jones, aged three. The posy was inscribed "From the remaining children of Aberfan".

The Times, October 30, 1966

The Queen and Prince Philip visit the coal-mining village of Aberfan following the disaster that resulted in the deaths of 116 children and 28 adults.

THE ROYAL GARDEN PARTY

by Daniel Finkelstein

"We do these things very well," my grandmother used to say when I was a boy and we watched a royal event on television. I thought it was a fitting comment; it seemed to me true, as far as I could make out from the telly, and I took pride in it.

Yet looking back, I think the most interesting word in the sentence was "we". My grandmother was born in Poland, as was my father. My mum was born in Berlin and brought up in Amsterdam. So it is interesting that the word "we" came naturally.

I think of King John as being part of my history, even though around the time of Magna Carta, my family was celebrating the crowning of Daniel of Galicia as King of Halych-Volhynia – give or take a hundred years or so.

I think this was part of the Queen's achievement, and her importance. She somehow made a diverse people – with an incredibly varied history – think of themselves as "we".

The royal garden party is one of the things my grandmother was talking about when she praised how we do things. I didn't experience it on television, however. I went.

It was almost 25 years ago now, while I was working for Conservative Central Office. I knew I hadn't been selected to go because of any special distinction. The office got some invitations and it was my turn. Still, it was nice to get the stiff, embossed card from the Lord Chamberlain. And I would definitely have put it on the mantelpiece if we'd had one. As it was, I left it nonchalantly on the radiator shelf, face up, just in case anyone came to mend the radiator and might be so impressed that they mended it more carefully.

When my wife and I arrived at Buckingham Palace, there was a queue to get in. Quite a long one. This was due to something I should have realised earlier. Indeed, I probably knew it, if I had been bothered to think it through.

Each party has many thousands of guests. About 8,000 each. Of course they do, or I would not have been invited.

However obvious and necessary this may be, it does, at first, seem a little disappointing. Yet as it turns out, it isn't a disappointing event. How could it be? Even walking across the gravel at the palace was exciting.

In order for a garden party to be anything other than a scrum, it has to be carefully organised. And fortunately, it is. Guests are encouraged to stand in lanes and a number are selected to meet members of the royal family. We were not, but because the Queen was meeting someone very close to where we were standing, we felt included in the conversation.

It was quite cleverly done. The whole royal family were present – the Queen Mother, for instance, was there – so you felt part of a special occasion, despite the number of guests. And after the lanes and collecting tea you could stroll round the gardens, which meant you weren't standing in a crowd the whole time.

Watching the Queen work was fascinating. Each encounter was a highlight in the life of the person she was meeting, while, for her, being just a few moments in the schedule.

These would have been moments that the visitor will never have forgotten but she would not have remembered even by suppertime. She had to do the same things, say the same things, over and over again.

Yet it never seemed like that. She was supremely professional, warm without being less than regal, interested without exhausting herself with small talk. I feel very fortunate to have been invited. The sense of being "we" is strong within me.

A garden party at the palace in 2012. About 8,000 guests attend each event.

FIT FOR A QUEEN
by Anna Murphy

"If I wore beige," the Queen once said, "nobody would know who I am." Dressed head to toe in cerise or turquoise, on the other hand, and there was no question as to who One was and there was no difficulty in picking One out in a crowd.

At heart, Her Majesty's sartorial choices were the regal equivalent of the hi-vis jacket, and often almost as bright. (Sunshine yellow has been a favourite shade since the 1980s.)

The Queen created her own sartorial rulebook. She had to; it's not as if there had been a recent precedent for a female British head of state when she succeeded her father in 1952.

Aside from her adherence to colour, she had strong views on hats, for example; above all that she wore one, and that the brim was off her face so it did not prevent the public getting a clear sightline.

She liked a two-inch block heel on her shoes (by Anello & Davide) to add height without sacrificing comfort. Her boxy patent bags (by Launer) were made with a slightly longer handle so they could be hooked over her forearm without catching on her cuff. Everything she wore or carried was custom made.

The Queen never saw fashion as a leveller; quite the reverse. Her 1947 wedding dress, for example, was an extravagant seed-pearl-and-crystal-encrusted Norman Hartnell creation. Some feared criticism as the wedding took place during postwar hardship and austerity but the public were delighted with their fairytale princess.

It was Hartnell she called on again to make her Coronation dress six years later, insisting that the floral symbols of Great Britain and the Commonwealth be incorporated, from Irish shamrocks to Canadian maple leaves. Those shamrocks reappeared – 2,091 of them this time – embroidered on the robe

Sunshine yellow was one of the Queen's favourite colours.

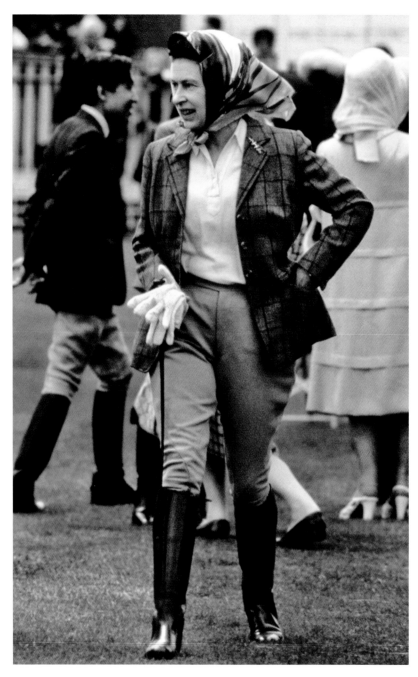

On less formal occasions the Queen preferred clothes that were more practical for her favourite pastimes, such as walking and riding.

she wore during her historic 2011 visit to Ireland. On royal tours the Queen consistently used her clothes to honour her host country.

So emblematic the Queen's mode of attire became over the years that you could see its influence on other women in the public eye, from Margaret Thatcher to Hillary Clinton. We didn't only recognise our Queen from her head on our stamps but from her signature ensembles.

When Elizabeth became Queen, she began working with Hartnell to develop a different look, eschewing her mother's fussier chiffons in favour of sleeker lines. She was a woman in a man's world and she needed to dress to be taken seriously, while still signalling her femininity.

She also came to rely upon Hardy Amies, who was celebrated for his subtle re-toolings of Parisian trends. In more recent years the majority of the Queen's wardrobe was created by Angela Kelly, who was served as her senior dresser from 2002. The daughter of a Liverpool dock worker, Kelly was also the Queen's personal assistant and close confidante.

Away from the public eye the Queen wore clothes that didn't get in the way of walking and riding: tweed skirts, lace-up brown shoes, sensible woollies, a headscarf, a raincoat. (She was Queen of the notoriously drizzly British Isles after all.) The colours she chose were those of our country, her country: earth, moss, heather, lichen. She wore a kind of camouflage. In her private life she could, at last, blend in.

The purples and blues.

The turquoises and greens.

The yellows and golds.

The oranges and pinks.

Hats ...

... and more hats.

The casual outfits.

The gowns.

RULING
PASSIONS

THE QUEEN AT HOME
by Hugo Vickers

At state banquets the goldplate comes out. The Queen was known to point out to state visitors that she did not live like that every day. In contrast, the Queen lived simply, even if on the outskirts of considerable grandeur. She enjoyed pleasures such as walking and feeding her dogs, and riding in the grounds at Windsor, Sandringham and Balmoral. Unlike Queen Elizabeth the Queen Mother, she was not personally extravagant.

She divided her time between four royal residences: Buckingham Palace, her official residence and what can be considered the monarch's main office; Windsor Castle, where she spent weekends in the Victorian Tower overlooking acres of garden, distant fields and woodland, and where she and Prince Philip shielded during the pandemic; Sandringham, the sprawling Edwardian mansion that was the place for Christmas and where the stud was based; and Balmoral, her gothic Victorian Scottish residence, the place for summers in the Highlands – and for the August weekend visit from the prime minister and their spouse.

At the palace, the Queen occupied – as during his lifetime did the Duke of Edinburgh – a long corridor on the Constitution Hill side of the building. The place has the feel of a rather grand Edwardian hotel. The duke, whose rooms once belonged to King George VI, had a library, a large drawing room, a smaller study, his bedroom and a bathroom.

The Queen's rooms were formerly used by her mother: an audience room, where she received formal visitors in some style, followed by her dining room where she dined if she didn't have an official engagement, a study sitting room (with a bow window), bedroom and dressing room. When the Queen was in her rooms, a page stood outside the door.

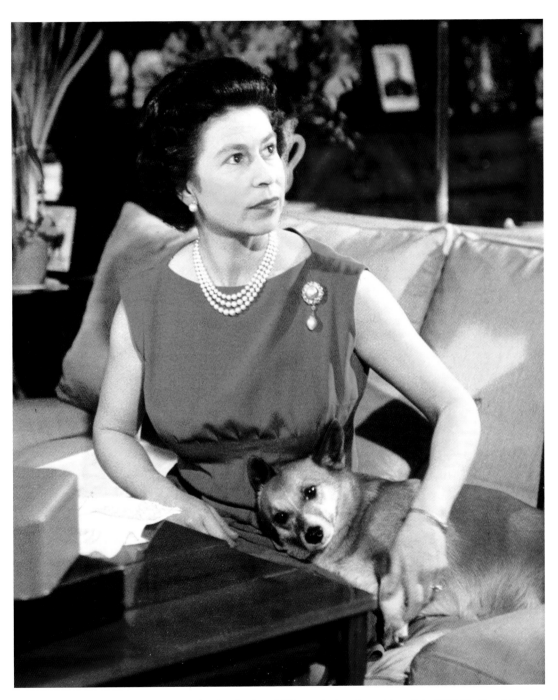

On the sofa with a corgi in 1969, in a still taken by Joan Williams during the making of the BBC film Royal Family.

We got occasional glimpses of the Queen in her private surroundings when she recorded her Christmas broadcast to the Commonwealth. Her rooms were formal and grand with fine furniture and paintings, and on every table there were photographs of her children, grandchildren and great-grandchildren, alongside signed photographs of foreign monarchs, many of them cousins. She had a private entrance into the garden, where footmen could be seen walking the corgis, when she could not do that herself.

At Windsor Castle, the Queen's private apartments, where she could make her own breakfast, overlooked the Long Walk. She liked to ride her pony and walk her dogs in the Home Park. The Countess of Wessex and her children often rode with her. On Sundays she drove herself to morning service in the Royal Chapel at Royal Lodge and sometimes went for post-matin drinks, for instance, before her death in 2016, with Margaret Rhodes, her cousin, or to another home in the park, such as the deputy ranger's.

At Easter, there was the Easter Court, when the Queen stayed at the castle for about three weeks. Guests – often the heads of charities or leading lights in their field – were invited to what is known as a "dine and sleep". They were shown to their rooms where their suitcases were unpacked. The Queen presided at a dinner party and afterwards there was often a tour of the royal library, where items were brought out, according to their interests. They said goodbye at the end of the evening. They didn't see her again the next morning and they left after breakfast.

The Queen spent the week after her official birthday in June at Windsor and, after entertaining the Knights and Ladies of the Garter on the Monday, she spent five days at Royal Ascot. Although this had a formal side with a carriage procession, she did not consider it a public duty: it was a pleasure. As such, it was perhaps the only occasion when, to some extent, she politely ignored other racegoers. Her interest was the horses.

For the Christmas break and occasionally in the summer she went to Sandringham. Here the atmosphere was similar to many country houses owned by the aristocracy – life was directed towards the outdoors.

The Queen took her summer holiday at Balmoral between July and October. Local landowners were invited to dinner and there was a succession of house guests – mainly family friends and relatives.

The Queen drove visitors around the estate in her Land Rover, or treated them to the traditional royal family "cook out". The duke used to conduct proceedings on a specially designed barbecue, which travelled in a trailer behind a Land Rover, with food and drink in compartments. It meant that the royal family could dispense with staff; the Queen liked to do the washing-up herself on these occasions.

The prime minister and their spouse were invited for a night at Balmoral at the end of August. This tended to coincide with the Braemar Games on the Saturday and a visit to Crathie church on the Sunday, at which the prime minister might read a lesson. A key event was the private audience with the Queen in her informal sitting room. Other than that, the visiting PM was expected to merge into the royal family's life, accompanying the Queen on a stroll around the kitchen garden, or perhaps visiting the Prince of Wales at Birkhall.

Entertaining prime ministers was a variable feast for the Queen, with stories that became the stuff of legend. Mrs Thatcher apparently tried to take over the washing-up after a barbecue. The Queen Mother happened to see Tony Blair and his wife arrive one year. Cherie was reluctant to curtsy, and the Queen Mother was heard to say: "Stiff knees, stiff knees." On the other hand, Gordon Brown was a more easy-going guest than his public persona would suggest.

Meanwhile, David Cameron recalled in his memoir how his visit to Balmoral was overshadowed by newspaper headlines at breakfast predicting that Scotland would vote to break up the Union, in the forthcoming referendum that Cameron himself had authorised.

The Queen and Prince Philip with their children at Sandringham in 1969,
from left: Edward, Anne, Charles and Andrew.

When at Balmoral the Queen usually wears tartan.
Here, she welcomes General Sir Peter Cosgrove, the Governor-General of Australia, to Balmoral Castle.

A QUEEN'S BEST FRIENDS

by Valentine Low

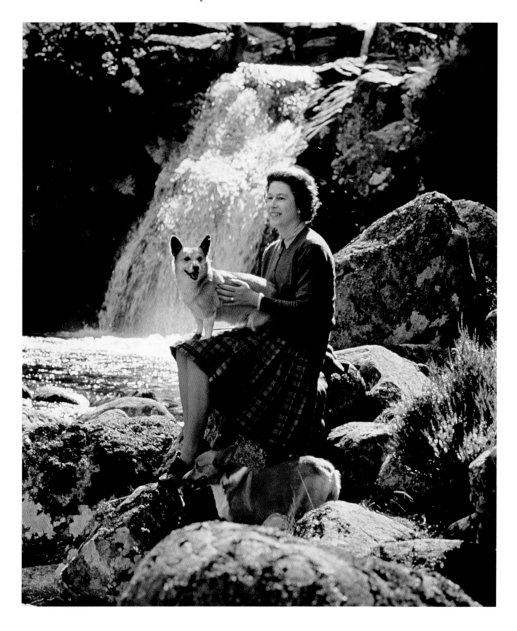

The Queen's corgis were an instantly recognisable part of her public image. From newspaper cartoons to the video she made with Daniel Craig for the 2012 London Olympics – in which the corgi Monty made a cameo appearance – when a corgi appeared, the Queen was never far behind. They even played a crucial role in kickstarting the plot in Alan Bennett's literary fantasy about the Queen, *The Uncommon Reader*.

Yet for all the Queen's devotion to her corgis – and her dorgis, a cross between a dachshund and a corgi – it would be wrong to think that she was a one-breed woman. There were labradors too, and spaniels: the Queen took an active interest in the Sandringham kennels, and in her prime was regarded as a highly proficient handler of gun dogs.

Her first dog, however, the one that inspired her love of animals, was none of these; it was a cairn terrier, given to her by her uncle, the Prince of Wales, the future Edward VIII. Princess Elizabeth was three years old at the time.

The first corgi to enter her life was called Dookie, bought by her father, George VI, in 1933. Others followed, generation after generation of them; one of the most notable was Susan, the matriarch of the dynasty. On the Queen's wedding day, when she and Prince Philip were driven in an open carriage from Buckingham Palace to Waterloo station for the start of their honeymoon, Susan travelled with them, snuggled up under a rug. At Waterloo she stole the show by tumbling out first on to the red carpet that awaited them.

Being a royal pet is, naturally, not a life short of privilege. At Buckingham Palace the dogs slept in their own room, in wicker baskets raised a few inches off the floor to avoid draughts. Whenever she could, the Queen exercised them herself, and it is said that if she was wearing a headscarf when she came into a room they sensed that a walk was imminent and would scamper about excitedly.

The former royal chef Darren McGrady, who worked for the Queen for 11 years, once described how the corgis would be served only the finest fare. "One day it would be chuck steak, which we boiled and served with finely chopped, boiled cabbage and white rice. The next they'd have poached chicken or liver. Or rabbits shot by William or Harry that we'd clean, cook, debone and chop for the dogs."

If the dogs could be unruly, it seemed to be just the way the Queen liked it. "They chase rabbits like mad," the Queen's cousin Margaret Rhodes said once. "There are a lot of rabbits around Balmoral, certainly, and the Queen gets excited with the dogs chasing the rabbits, egging them on. Telling them to keep going – 'Keep on going!'" There could be trouble, though. Susan once bit the royal clock winder, and also attacked one of the palace sentries. Another dog bit a policeman.

There were reports in later years that the Queen was starting not to replace her dogs as they died. Monty Roberts, an informal adviser to the Queen, said in 2014 that she had declined his offer to find a puppy after the death of Monty. He told *Vanity Fair* magazine: "She didn't want any more young dogs. She didn't want to leave any young dog behind. She wanted to put an end to it."

While Prince Philip was ill in hospital in 2021, however, she was given a pair of puppies by Prince Andrew. She apparently viewed Muick and Fergus – named after her mother's brother, who was killed in the First World War – as a welcome distraction, particularly once she was grieving for her husband. Unhappily, Fergus died shortly after as well, but she still walked Muick, a corgi, together with another dorgi, Candy.

Princess Elizabeth and Princess Margaret with the dogs in the Little House – their two-thirds size cottage in the grounds of the Royal Lodge, Windsor – in 1936.

Queen Elizabeth walking the dogs on the Balmoral estate, along with Prince Philip, Princess Anne and Prince Charles.

The Queen at the Royal Windsor Horse Show, 1973.

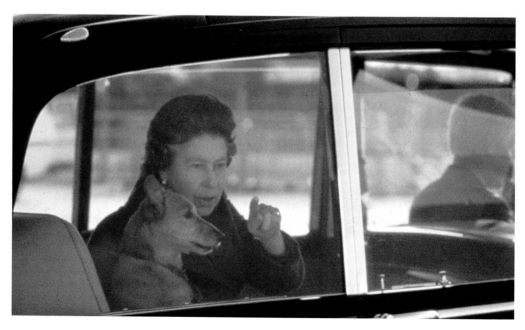

The Queen chats to one of her pets on her return from Balmoral in 1986.

The Queen arrives at Aberdeen airport with a trio of dogs, ready to start her holiday in Balmoral in 1974.

SPORT OF QUEENS

by Julian Muscat

On the morning of her Coronation, Princess Elizabeth was asked by a lady-in-waiting how she was feeling. She replied that she was very well: her trainer had just called to relate that her horse Aureole had completed his Derby preparation with a pleasing gallop.

Four days later, on her first visit to Epsom, she watched in a state of high excitement as Aureole finished runner-up to Pinza. Aureole's noble effort was still the closest she came to winning the Derby. Her inaugural win in a Classic came four years later, when her homebred filly Carrozza took the Oaks at Epsom, ridden by Lester Piggott.

The Queen's relationship with racing was not so much a casual acquaintance as a full-blooded embrace. Racecourses were her sanctuary, where she could be herself. She was often at Newbury's spring meeting in April, when she was in her element. Unlike the Derby or Ascot, where she was invariably a focal point, here the Queen would simply dissolve into the mix. She moved around without overt security. She could be like any other owner as she assessed runners in the paddock before making her way through crowds towards the grandstand. During her visits to the races the Queen radiated happiness, in contrast to her oft-sombre appearance in the line of duty.

She would doubtless have spent more time on the racecourse if circumstances had permitted. She once mused that but for the Archbishop of Canterbury she would have been off in her plane every Sunday to Longchamp, in Paris, where her filly Highclere galloped to victory in the 1974 Prix de Diane.

If her zest for racing was plain, she revealed more about herself when visiting her horses at her trainers' stables. She wanted no fuss; she wanted only to see her thoroughbreds going through their paces. Her insistence on informality encouraged her trainers to treat her in kind. Most of them did just that – especially Richard Hannon, who served her for 16 years until his retirement in 2013, and whose jovial insouciance the Queen found particularly amusing.

Her love of racing surfaced spontaneously, as it did in 2008, when her horse Free Agent ended a nine-year royal drought at Ascot. There the Queen stood, punching the air before hot-footing it down to the winner's enclosure. "It was as if she was 20 years old," recalled her bloodstock and racing adviser John Warren, who succeeded his father-in law, the 7th Earl of Carnarvon, to the post on the latter's death in 2001. "The rest of us were struggling to keep up."

Warren was well placed to amplify the Queen's passion. "It didn't take me long to realise that her fundamental interest revolves utterly and totally around the horse itself," he said. "The depth of her knowledge is extraordinary. Nobody else in the country has been breeding racehorses for more than 60 years."

Princess Elizabeth was three years old when George V regaled his granddaughter with the story of Scuttle carrying the royal silks to victory in the 1928 One Thousand Guineas at Newmarket. A year later she was given Peggy, her first pony. However, her love of racing escalated in 1942, when her father owned a pair of superior racehorses whose exploits would bring him the accolade of Britain's leading owner.

In the spring of that year George VI took his daughter to Fred Darling's stables in Beckhampton, Wiltshire, to cast her eye over Big Game and Sun Chariot. The two horses would win four of the five Classics and Princess Elizabeth, then 16, was so smitten on touching their silken coats that she would not wash her hands for hours afterwards.

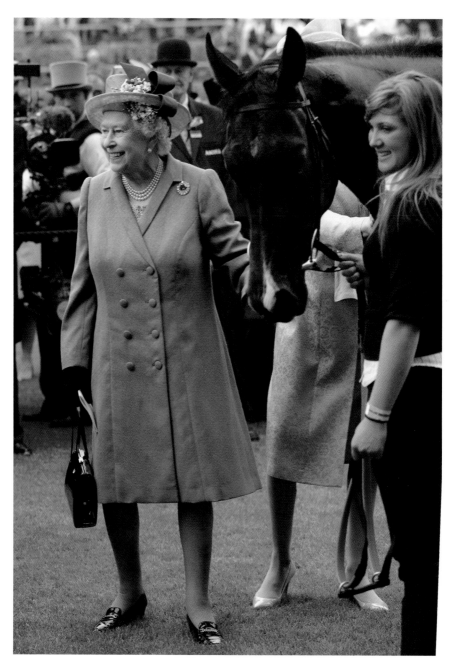

The Queen with her horse, Estimate, who galloped to victory in the Gold Cup of 2013 at Royal Ascot.

To the public, the Queen was synonymous with Royal Ascot. She hosted a lunch at Windsor Castle on each of the meeting's five days and was always anxious to arrive at the racecourse punctually. She savoured 24 Royal Ascot winners in the distinctive purple and red royal silks, among them Expansive in the 1979 Ribblesdale Stakes, a race she won three times.

They came thick and fast in the early years, when the Royal Studs were not in competition with the plethora of Middle Eastern potentates who have patronised British racing since the early 1980s. There were limits to what she could spend on bloodstock: the royal horses were all paid for from the Queen's private purse. Nevertheless, despite front-line successes becoming increasingly elusive, the Queen's interest intensified with the passing years.

In her early eighties she decided to overhaul bloodlines within the Royal Studs, a decision which in time led to fresh conquests. For the Queen, however, it was not all about the big occasion. It was about giving every one of her horses the best possible opportunity to express its potential.

Her biggest triumph to date came in 2013 when Estimate galloped away with Royal Ascot's signature race, the Gold Cup. It marked the first victory for a British monarch in the race's 207-year history, after which the Queen revealed that it was the race she had yearned to win above all others.

The Queen leads in her filly Carrozza after it won the Oaks at Epsom in 1957, ridden by Lester Piggott.

*Congratulating her horse Expansive, which won the Ribblesdale Stakes
at Ascot in 1979, with Lord Carnarvon (right).*

With her racing manager John Warren on Derby Day at Epsom in 2012,
the first day of her four-day Diamond Jubilee celebrations.

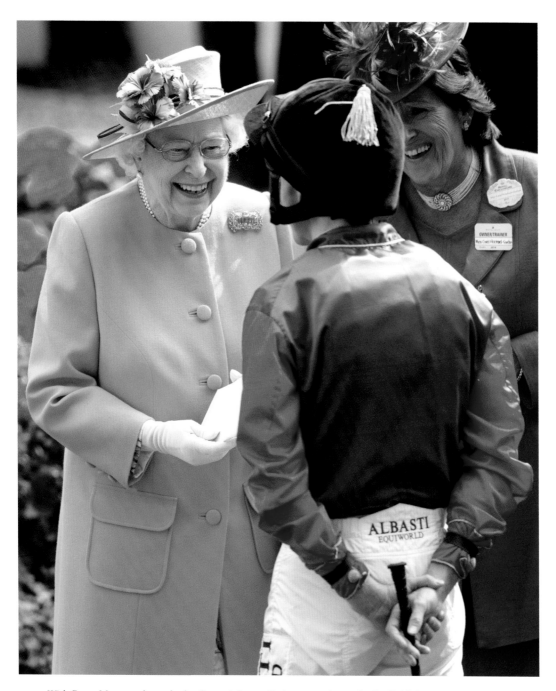

With Ryan Moore, who rode the Queen's horse Estimate to victory in the Gold Cup at Ascot in 2013.

A
FAMILY AFFAIR

THE ROYAL TRIUMVIRATE

by Hugo Vickers

No women were closer to the Queen than her mother and sister. At first they had been a family of four – King George VI, Queen Elizabeth and the two princesses. The King was concerned that the "us four" arrangement would end when Princess Elizabeth married Prince Philip in 1947 as, inevitably, it did.

The dynamics changed again when the King died in 1952. The Queen Mother had been virtually acting head of state while the King had been gravely ill. Now she was to change from being a supporting wife to leading life on her own terms – a mixture of the diplomatic, ambassadorial and social.

Throughout her life, however, she remained a quiet force behind the Queen. They talked regularly on the telephone, they went to church at weekends in Windsor, she stayed in the castle for Ascot week and spent time with her daughter at Sandringham. The Queen deferred to her mother in many ways on private family occasions – for example, giving her the King's seat in the chapel at Royal Lodge (in Windsor Great Park) for Sunday matins.

She always allowed her mother a BAE 146 aircraft to travel in if she needed it, while this privilege was not automatically granted to Princess Margaret or to other members of the royal family. She did not rein in her mother's perceived extravagances, the Queen Mother believing that she should continue to occupy four residences – Clarence House in London, Royal Lodge at Windsor, Birkhall on the Balmoral estate and the privately owned Castle of Mey in Thurso, in the far north of Scotland. At all of them she entertained extensively.

The Queen continued to run royal life much as in her father's day, out of respect for his memory and to please her mother. Inevitably changes had to be gradually introduced. It was always hinted that the royal family might give up Sandringham, their country estate in Norfolk, but that the Queen Mother would never have approved.

As the Queen Mother reached extreme old age, there is no doubt that she caused the Queen considerable worry by refusing to slow down. The Queen bought her a mobility buggy, decorated in her racing colours, but for some years the Queen Mother refused to use it. At the end of a ball to celebrate her golden wedding in 1997, the Queen was heard to say: "I'm trying to persuade Mummy to go to bed." The Queen Mother was 97 at the time. While the public looked on admiringly as the Queen Mother walked the length of the aisle of St Paul's Cathedral at the age of 100, the Queen was anxious that her mother might fall in public.

The death of the Queen Mother in March 2002, at the age of 101, while the cause of sorrow and reflection, also relieved the Queen of considerable stress. As she undertook her Golden Jubilee engagements, she looked more relaxed, began to dress more stylishly, and in a sense asserted her personality in a new way. For many years, the Queen Mother had drawn the affection of the nation to her by her outgoing and generous personality. Only in 2002 did the Queen herself finally, albeit quietly, assume the role of royal matriarch.

The Queen was also very close to Princess Margaret and was frequently concerned about her sister's happiness. They had spent their childhood together, been inseparable during the war and only slightly distanced by the Queen's marriage in 1947.

Margaret Whitlam, the wife of the Australian prime minister, Gough Whitlam, stayed at Windsor Castle in April 1973 and captured something of the relationship between the Queen and Princess Margaret: "You would have loved the sight of the sisters sitting side by side on the deep-piled cream sheepskin rug we gave Her Majesty for her birthday. They looked like 'the Little Princesses' on either one's teenage birthday." She also recorded that the Queen and her sister indulged in proficient imitations – "gentle send-ups" – of people around them, including the Queen Mother.

There were many occasions on which the Queen's public position as monarch clashed with her private feelings. As early as 1953 there was the question of Princess Margaret marrying a divorced equerry, Group Captain Peter Townsend, a man much liked by the Queen and by the Queen Mother. The Queen's private hopes for her sister's happiness were thrown into conflict with her role as head of the Church of England, which at that time was sternly hostile to divorce.

Princess Margaret did not have her mother's resilience. Whereas the Queen Mother never disappointed the British public, Princess Margaret was more capricious. She did not aim to please and win over people in the way the Queen Mother did. The royal family were surprised when Princess Margaret married Antony Armstrong-Jones (later Viscount Snowdon), a photographer, in 1960.

The marriage was happy at first but ultimately unravelled. Their separation in 1976 and divorce in 1978 was a time of great sadness and upheaval in Princess Margaret's life and she received the Queen's moral support. In the mid-1990s, Princess Margaret's life settled on to a more even keel with the marriages of her children and the arrival of grandchildren, but then her health broke down.

Devoted as the Queen was to her mother and sister, their deaths, within a few weeks of each other in 2002, released her from pressure and anxiety. Inevitably, she minded Princess Margaret's death more. She had been the companion of her childhood, four years younger, and she missed a forceful, animated and spirited person.

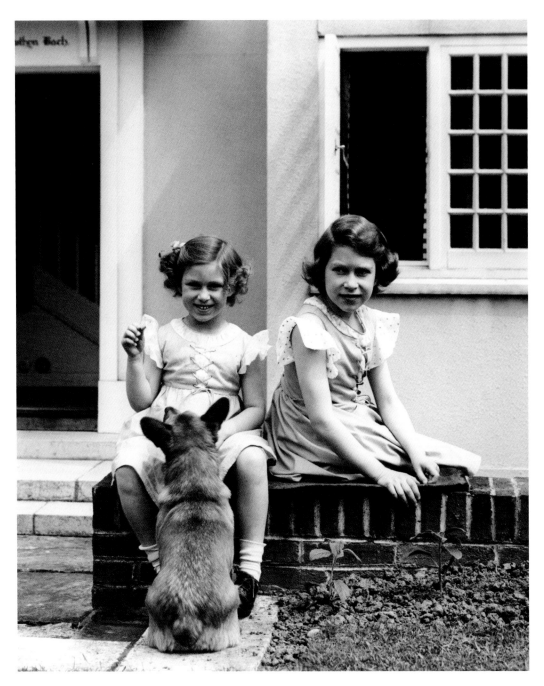

Princess Margaret and Princess Elizabeth playing with the family dogs.

The Queen Mother – pictured here with Princess Margaret and the Queen – refused to slow down in her old age.

The Queen celebrates the Queen Mother's 80th birthday with Princess Margaret on August 4, 1980.

THE QUEEN'S CHILDREN
by Sally Bedell Smith

When she became Queen at the age of 25, Elizabeth was already the mother of three-year-old Prince Charles and 18-month-old Princess Anne. Her one maternal adjustment to what had been her father's routine as King was to change the time for the weekly audience with the prime minister from 5.30pm to 6.30pm. This allowed her to join her children in the nursery for their nightly bath and bedtime.

Thus began a lifetime of combining service to her country with her role as a parent, every bit of it under a scrutinising, often critical public eye. Like any mother, she had her share of missteps, dramas and rifts with her children. Like all children, they turned out not quite as she might have expected or planned.

Yet if one moment sums up Elizabeth's legacy as a mother and the reciprocal love of her children, it was during the Diamond Jubilee concert in 2012, when Charles addressed her in front of 18,000 people on a grandstand outside Buckingham Palace, and a further half a million watching on large screens in St James's Park, The Mall and Hyde Park. "Your Majesty – Mummy," he said, drawing an unusually huge public smile from her, and great cheers from the crowd. Then he thanked her "for inspiring us with your selfless duty and service, and for making us proud to be British". They were sentiments that he would echo again in his first speech as King.

From the outset of her reign, Elizabeth felt it essential to demonstrate her gravitas to the older men (and they were all men) who advised her. As a career woman, she was an anomaly in her generation and in the British upper class, combining the roles of monarch, wife and mother without any ready role model. She waited ten years before having her third child, Prince Andrew, and four years later Prince Edward was born, in 1964.

"Nothing, but nothing, deflected her from duty," recalled Sir Edward Ford, an assistant private secretary to the Queen. "She'd go into labour and have a baby, so we knew we weren't going to see her for a while.

The new Queen, Princess Anne and Prince Charles at Balmoral in 1952.

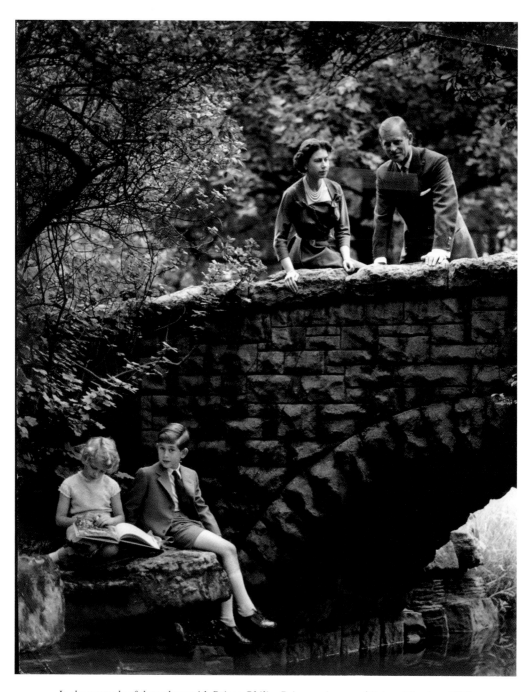

In the grounds of the palace with Prince Philip, Princess Anne and Prince Charles, 1957.

The Queen salutes with two-day-old Prince Edward in her arms and four-year-old Prince Andrew next to her on the palace balcony during Trooping the Colour in 1964.

Prince Philip, Prince Edward, the Queen, Prince Andrew, Princess Anne and Prince Charles in the grounds of Frogmore, on the Windsor estate, in 1968.

But within a very short time, 24 or 48 hours at most, she'd be asking whether there were any papers and would we care to send them up?" She took overseas trips as well; her first extensive tour of Commonwealth countries in 1953 and 1954 kept her away from Charles and Anne for nearly six months.

Her children were fortunate to have a nurturing nanny in Mabel Anderson, who was only a year younger than the Queen and had an affectionate and flexible nature as well as a firm sense of right and wrong. Their maternal grandmother, the Queen Mother, was also an important force who particularly doted on Prince Charles – sometimes to the point of cosseting.

Clarissa Eden, the wife of the then prime minister Anthony Eden (later the 1st Earl of Avon), was perplexed that the Queen and the Queen Mother failed to discipline six-year-old Charles during a picnic at Windsor Castle when he refused to yield his chair to the prime minister. Lady Avon was surprised that the Queen "didn't say, 'Come on, Charles, get up,' but I suppose she doesn't like scenes at all costs".

All her children knew that she spent long hours in her office at Buckingham Palace, where her priorities were, as Prince Andrew put it, "work and responsibilities and duties". While the Queen certainly loved her children, she fell into professional habits that pulled her away from motherhood. As a result, she missed out on many maternal challenges as well as pleasures. "She let things go," said Gay Charteris, the wife of the Queen's long-time private secretary Martin Charteris. "She did have work every day. It was easier to go back to that than children having tantrums. She always had the excuse of the red boxes." "She was not a hugger," agreed the Queen's first cousin, Lady Mary Clayton. "She has a different nature. There is a self-containment."

The Queen was more visibly engaged with her second set of children. When Mabel Anderson took time off, the Queen felt relaxed enough to stay in the nursery with Andrew and Edward, tying on an apron for their baths and lulling them to sleep.

During weekends at Windsor Castle, the boys zoomed down the gilded Grand Corridor in their pedal cars, and if they fell off their bicycles on one of the gravel paths in the park, the Queen would "pick them up and say, 'Don't be so silly. There's nothing wrong with you. Go and wash off' just like any parent," Prince Andrew recalled. At teatime, she joined them to watch the BBC's *Grandstand* sports programme on Saturdays and the Sunday cricket league.

All four children found common ground with both parents during their holidays at the family's rural estates, Sandringham in Norfolk and Balmoral in Aberdeenshire. The Queen and Prince Philip taught their children to appreciate their natural surroundings and instructed them how to shoot as well as how to cast into the pools of the River Dee and catch salmon with a well-tied fly. They stalked stag with their parents at Balmoral, and they spent hours on horseback across what Anne remembered as the "miles of stubble fields around Sandringham" and among "the autumn colours of the rowans and silver birches, the majesties of the old Scots pines" at Balmoral.

It was perhaps here, away from the pressures of duty, that the Queen was able to bond best with her children, and where she was most able to be herself. In more recent decades, the Queen cultivated a love of country pursuits in her grandchildren too. By the time they were teenagers, Prince William and Prince Harry were regulars on the Scottish grouse moors and at Sandringham for pheasant shoots. Edward, the Earl of Wessex, is a keen shot and attends shoots at Sandringham with his son James, Viscount Severn, now in his teens.

The press of her duties prompted the Queen to make her husband the ultimate arbiter in decisions about their children. She believed Prince Philip's role as head of the family was "the natural state of things". He enforced discipline, and he selected their children's schools, which in the case of Charles reflected Philip's belief in the merit of his own experience rather than what was appropriate for his diffident, sensitive and awkward eldest son.

Charles hated Gordonstoun, the boarding school in Scotland that he found severe, although his younger brothers fared better, not least because by then the atmosphere was more humane with the inclusion of girls. Princess Anne, whose self-confidence and assertiveness mirrored her father's personality, did well at Benenden, her boarding school in Kent.

Particularly with her two eldest children, Charles and Anne, the Queen believed in the necessity of exposing them to challenging situations and talking to them "on level grown-up terms". "I remember the patience Prince Charles showed when he was around all those adults,'" said Mary Wilson, the wife of the Labour prime minister Harold Wilson. The royal children may have grown up in a bubble, but the Queen wanted them to work through difficulties and learn to think for themselves. "I learnt the way a monkey learns – by watching its parents," Charles once said.

During Anne's trip to New Zealand with her parents in 1970, the "walkabout" was introduced into the royal routine, a casual stroll to chat and shake hands with ordinary people. "At 19 years old, suddenly being dropped in the middle of the street," Anne recalled. "Suddenly being told to pick someone and talk to them. Fun? No, I don't think so."

Anne had a strong bond with her mother through horses, especially when she became a top competitor in the arduous equestrian sport of three-day eventing. She was married at a young age, in 1973, to Captain Mark Phillips, an accomplished horseman who won an Olympic gold medal.

Andrew distinguished himself as a helicopter pilot who saw combat during the Falklands conflict in 1982. On his return after more than five months away, the Queen appeared to wipe tears from her eyes during the flag-waving homecoming at Portsmouth, as her second son greeted her with a red rose between his teeth. She was genuinely pleased in 1986 when he married Sarah Ferguson, a robust and jolly young woman who shared the monarch's love of riding and other country pursuits.

Edward, who had his mother's shy streak, struggled after earning his degree at Cambridge. He first bailed out of training as a Royal Marine and then stumbled in trying to establish himself as a film producer. He finally found his footing when he teamed up with his father in running the Duke of Edinburgh's awards for young people. Edward's much later marriage, at the age of 35, to Sophie Rhys-Jones, a middle-class public relations consultant, drew him closer to his mother.

"Sophie first of all respects her as the Queen, then as a mother-in-law, but she also understands that she is a human being and treats her that way," observed the Queen's cousin, Lady Elizabeth Anson.

The Queen "allowed Prince Charles to work at his interests, his aims and his ambitions" said Sir Malcolm Ross, one of her senior advisers. "It is not a cosy relationship," said the Queen's cousin Margaret Rhodes. "They love each other, but the family is not set up to be cosy."

The absence of cosiness made her children's marital break-ups much more difficult for the Queen to recognise and understand, especially with Charles and Diana, Princess of Wales. "I think it took a long time to accept that the faults were not more his than hers," said Patricia Mountbatten, her third cousin. In 1992 – what the Queen called her "annus horribilis" when Anne, Charles and Andrew split from their spouses – she found it all "nonplussing", recalled Mountbatten. "You don't know how to behave when someone is making such a mess. You want to help them mend, but how to do it?"

The publication in 1994 of Prince Charles's officially sanctioned biography drove a wedge between the heir and his parents. The author Jonathan Dimbleby quoted his complaints that the Queen had been remote during his unhappy childhood and that Philip had been overbearing and insensitive. His parents were wounded and his three siblings were indignant and rebuked Charles to his face.

A decade later, after another book that elaborated on these themes, Princess Anne countered that "it just beggars belief" to suggest that her mother was aloof and uncaring, adding that she and her brothers "understood what the limitations were in time and the responsibilities placed on her". Anne said they all appreciated being "allowed to find our own way ... People have to make their own mistakes. I think she's always accepted that."

The Queen steered the monarchy steadily across the decades, reinforcing its place as the linchpin of the country's identity even as she moved subtly with the times. More fundamentally, however, she presided over a modern and effective royal family, despite the hiccups along the way.

As in any family, these will always occur, the most significant of recent times being the rift with the Sussexes – Harry and Meghan – and the fall-out from Andrew's association with Jeffrey Epstein, the sex offender, which in 2019 led to the Duke of York retreating from his public duties, and losing military titles and royal patronages in January 2022.

After decades of turbulence, the Queen's other children have settled down, found happiness and worked hard to earn the admiration and affection of the people. With their visible commitment to public service and fulfilment of their royal duties, it is clear that their mother trained them well, instilling in them the values and traditions essential to the institution she led so brilliantly for 70 years.

*Driving in Windsor in 1957, with Prince Charles and Princess Anne
in the passenger seats to the delight of onlookers.*

With Prince Charles, Prince Edward and Prince Andrew at the Montreal Olympics, July 1976.

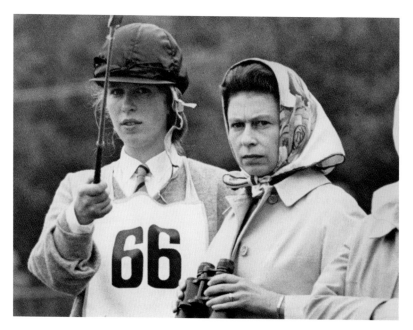

At the 1968 Eridge Horse Trials in East Sussex, where Princess Anne was competing.

Explaining the finer points of Trooping the Colour to Prince Edward at Buckingham Palace, c 1972.

THE QUEEN AND DIANA

by Valentine Low

In one of the most memorable, if not exactly subtle, scenes in the 2006 film *The Queen*, after the death of Diana, Princess of Wales, Helen Mirren comes face to face with a magnificent lone deer that, after a long stare, she shoos away in an attempt to save its life.

Whether this captured the Queen's view of Diana is questionable; after all, it was in fact Diana's brother, Charles Spencer, who called her the most hunted person of the modern age. While sympathetic, the Queen also thought her daughter-in-law behaved badly; she never understood her.

It was always her attitude not to try to cause trouble, a tendency that showed itself when Prince Charles was considering marrying Diana. While the Queen Mother was strongly in favour, the Queen, according to Charles's biographer Jonathan Dimbleby, "characteristically ... refrained from tendering her opinion".

While Charles and the palace machine never really knew what to do with Diana, the Queen was never less than supportive. The problem, perhaps, was that she was never anything more than supportive either. Diana revered the Queen but the aura that surrounded her, together with the Queen's natural reserve, meant that they never achieved anything like intimacy.

As early as her honeymoon, Diana had the capacity to leave the Queen baffled. At Balmoral, when she had a fit of sulks and refused to come down to dinner, the Queen was mystified as to how someone could behave so badly.

While the Queen is said to have liked the glamour Diana brought to the monarchy, it gave her daughter-in-law a power she quickly learnt to use. As relations with Charles went from bad to worse the Queen found herself increasingly torn over how to react.

The Princess of Wales and the Queen at the state opening of parliament in 1982.

The Queen preferred not to intervene in Charles and Diana's troubled marriage.

Diana recounted how whenever the subject of her marriage came up, the Queen would look worried and twiddle her glasses in her hands. Later, according to her lover James Hewitt, Diana summoned up the courage to have a frank discussion with her mother-in-law about her problems. "The Queen promised she would do what she could to take some pressure off her, and newspaper editors were asked not to subject her to too much scrutiny," said Hewitt. "But when it came to the issue of her marriage to Charles, the Queen said there was nothing she could do. It would be wrong to intervene."

The Queen did her best to remain neutral: whatever Diana had done, she and Philip also disapproved of Charles's own infidelity with Camilla Parker Bowles (as she was). However, when the Queen wrote to say that divorce was in the country's best interests, Diana was furious.

The Queen's failure to understand Diana became, after her death in a car accident in Paris in 1997, a failure to understand the nation's grief. She stayed in Balmoral, thinking it was best for her grandsons; the people thought otherwise. Nearly a week later, she briefly appeared in The Mall to look at flowers and later addressed the country.

Speaking "as your Queen and as a grandmother", she called Diana "an exceptional and gifted human being" and said there were "lessons to be drawn from her life and from the extraordinary and moving reaction to her death".

The Duke of Edinburgh and the Queen survey the floral tributes to Diana on The Mall, 1997.

A NEW
ELIZABETHAN AGE

A TRUE ANNUS HORRIBILIS

by Valentine Low

On November 24, 1992, the Queen had a heavy cold. It had been exacerbated by the smoke from the fire that devastated Windsor Castle and it gave added poignancy to a speech she made at Guildhall marking her 40 years on the throne.

"Nineteen ninety-two is not a year on which I shall look back with undiluted pleasure," she said. "In the words of one of my more sympathetic correspondents, it has turned out to be an 'Annus Horribilis'."

It had, indeed, been a terrible year for the royal family: as well as the fire, the marriages of the Queen's three eldest children were all in the process of collapse. Perhaps more importantly the speech marked a turning point in the royal family's relationship with the British people. Bleak in both content and delivery, with its talk of how no institution could expect to be free from scrutiny, the speech was either an appeal for forbearance and understanding or an act of penitence.

It was also a heavy hint of what was to come only two days later. In the Commons, John Major, the prime minister, announced that the following year the Queen and the Prince of Wales would start paying tax on their private income, and that £900,000 of Civil List payments to other members of the royal family would come to an end.

Of the three marriage breakdowns, at least the Queen knew one was coming: the divorce of Princess Anne and Mark Phillips, who had been separated for some years, was finalised in April. The tabloids were rarely short of tittle-tattle from the other two. In January, photographs were published of the Duchess of York on holiday with her Texan friend Steve Wyatt. Six days later the duke and duchess decided to separate.

The Prince and Princess of Wales, meanwhile, were conducting a highly public marital war. However, nothing prepared people for the shock of the serialisation in *The Sunday Times* in June of Andrew Morton's book *Diana: Her True Story*.

Readers learnt how Diana had deliberately thrown herself down the stairs at Sandringham, and had even slashed her wrists with a razor blade. Her bulimia and depression were charted in devastating detail. While Diana was portrayed as vulnerable and unable to cope, Charles was castigated for his lack of understanding and his relationship with Camilla Parker Bowles.

The Queen was both furious and deeply troubled by it all. In her biography of the Queen, Sarah Bradford painted a vivid picture of the awkward atmosphere at Royal Ascot that year, with Prince Philip refusing to talk to Diana and the Queen in "a pretty bad temper", according to one of her guests.

The scandals kept on coming. In August, the *Daily Mirror* published a picture of the Duchess of York topless by a pool as her friend and so-called financial adviser, John Bryan, kissed her toes. *The Sun* published the transcript of a telephone conversation between Diana and James Gilbey, in which he called her "Squidgy" and she described her marriage as "torture". Another recording surfaced in November, courtesy of *The Sun*. This time it was the Prince of Wales and Camilla Parker Bowles, and featured the prince uttering such toe-curling endearments as "Your great achievement is to love me."

Discontent about the royals' tax affairs rumbled on. Behind the scenes, moves were already afoot to address the tax question. In public, however, it looked as if the royal family was on the back foot, with both Labour and Tory MPs calling for reform.

Then, on November 20, fire broke out at Windsor Castle after a restorer's lamp set a curtain alight. St George's Hall suffered extensive damage, along with the state dining room and three drawing rooms. Although there was sympathy for the royals, in a woeful misreading of the public mood, the heritage secretary Peter Brooke announced that as the castle was uninsured, the government would foot the repair bill, estimated at the time to be £60 million. The restoration was later paid for without any recourse to public funds.

On December 9 came the announcement of the separation of the Prince and Princess of Wales. Days later, *The Sun* published the text of the Queen's Christmas broadcast before it went out. The Queen successfully sued for breach of copyright. It would take time, however, before the royal family's standing recovered.

Fire swept through Windsor Castle in November 1992.

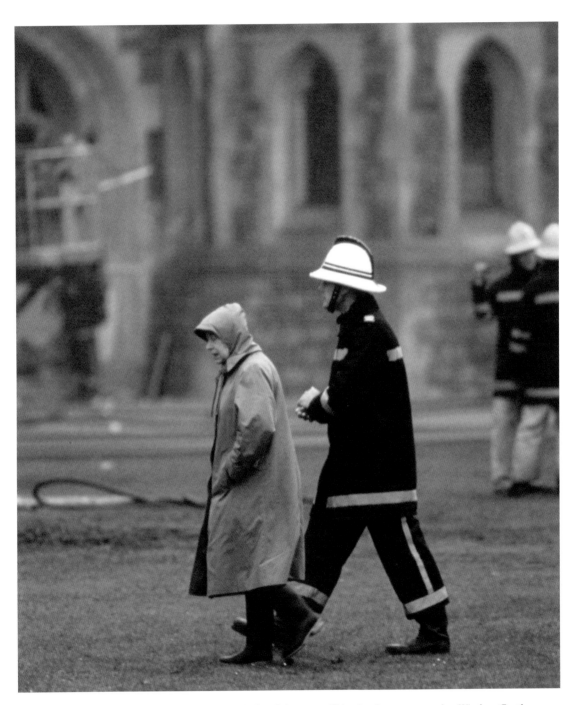

Prince Andrew said the Queen was "shocked and devastated" by the damage caused to Windsor Castle.

~ The Queen Shares ~ Her Sadness

The Queen returned to London to face her people yesterday, and they left her in no doubt that she was welcome.

At two public appearances she looked at times red-eyed and only just within the bounds of composure, at times astonished at the mountains of flowers and the size of the crowds and, in brief flashes of smile, relieved that any mild criticism of the Crown displaying insufficient public mourning seemed to have been forgiven by her presence.

As the Queen and the Duke of Edinburgh arrived from Balmoral at the Buckingham Palace gates, they got out of the car to look at the flowers and tributes to her late former daughter-in-law draped along the entire frontage. Turning to her husband, she shook her head as she pointed to the carpet of floral tributes. She saw too a poignant reminder of recent disquiet: a small Union Flag at half-mast left by one of the many thousands who had come to grieve.

Slowly the Queen walked along the lines of flowers, occasionally leaning down to read a message, pointing out a child's toy or a memorable photograph to Prince Philip.

She looked moved by the unforeseen and unprecedented expression of public grief. For several moments the royal couple stood together, heads bowed, lost in thought at the thousands of handwritten tributes, many of which were critical of their monarch.

As the crowd realised the Queen was walking among the flowers, they broke into applause. She turned for a second, smiled then returned to gaze on the endless succession of simple tributes. She told one woman: "I never realised there had been so many flowers left; it is remarkable."

Dressed in black with a simple hat and three strings of pearls, the Queen spent ten minutes walking back and forth before the crowd, with bouquets pressed into her hands and those of the Duke at almost every step.

Before she retired back into the palace she turned to look down The Mall, by now a sea of faces almost as far as she could see. However much her advisers had briefed her on the events and the mood in London, she was patently unprepared for the sheer size of the public expressions of sympathy for the Princess.

The story was the same at St. James's Palace, where the Queen and the Duke spent 15 minutes privately in the Chapel Royal, where the body of the Princess lies before the altar under Holbein's painted ceiling commemorating Henry VIII's brief marriage to Anne of Cleves. As she emerged from the palace, a waiting crowd of thousands broke into applause. Briefly, the Queen smiled, and went straight to another spontaneous display of flowers on the pavement. She made for the head of the queue, still hundreds of yards long, that for five days has shuffled towards the books of condolence.

Fred Cultworthy, 44, pressed a single rose in her hand. "I bought it for Diana, but I gave it to the Queen so that she would not think everybody thought the same way as some newspapers," he said.

Laura Trant, 15, said: "We told her how sorry we were, and we told her to look after the boys. She said 'I will'. She couldn't believe how hard it was for them because they were so young. Her mouth was quivering and her eyes were tearful."

As the Queen walked the first hundred yards of the queue, many others expressed their feelings about the young princes. She told one woman: "The boys are the important thing."

Beryl Holliday, 54, was glad to have spoken to the Queen. "Everybody here thinks it was worth the wait. I hope she has listened to the people."

The Times, September 6, 1997

Princess Diana's family watch the hearse depart at her funeral on September 6, 1997.

REINVENTING THE MONARCHY

by Damian Whitworth

The moment during her reign when the Queen's ability to reinvent the monarchy for the modern age was demonstrated most cleverly came when she starred as a Bond girl. Her agreement to participate in the opening ceremony of the 2012 Olympic Games with Daniel Craig was a masterstroke. As she and 007 appeared to parachute into the stadium, the audience let out a gasp audible to the ceremony's television audience of 900 million. The six-minute film, showing the Queen and Craig in the grandeur of Buckingham Palace, then their stunt doubles throwing themselves out of a helicopter above the stadium, was a fusion of ancient royal mystique with modern wit.

The Queen's reign spanned the TV age but she would not have considered anything as bold even a few years earlier. That she could provide the biggest surprise on a night of theatrical wonders was testimony to how shrewdly she had led the steady rebranding of "The Firm" after years when the share price had been heavily depressed.

In 2012, her Diamond Jubilee year, the Queen's approval ratings reached new heights. Ninety per cent of Britons said they were satisfied with how she did her job. Only 7 per cent said they were dissatisfied – the sort of figures of which elected heads of state can only dream. This marked a significant upturn in her popularity from the tumultuous 1990s when the monarchy reeled from one crisis to another, the public began to take a dim view and there was a rise in republican sentiment.

From those dark days the Queen spearheaded a remarkable comeback in the fortunes of her family, showing the monarchy's ability to evolve, and securing its place in the future of these islands. As *The Times* put it during the Diamond Jubilee: "It is easy to forget, in the summer of 2012, that half a generation ago the royal house of Windsor had stretched the people's patience close to breaking point."

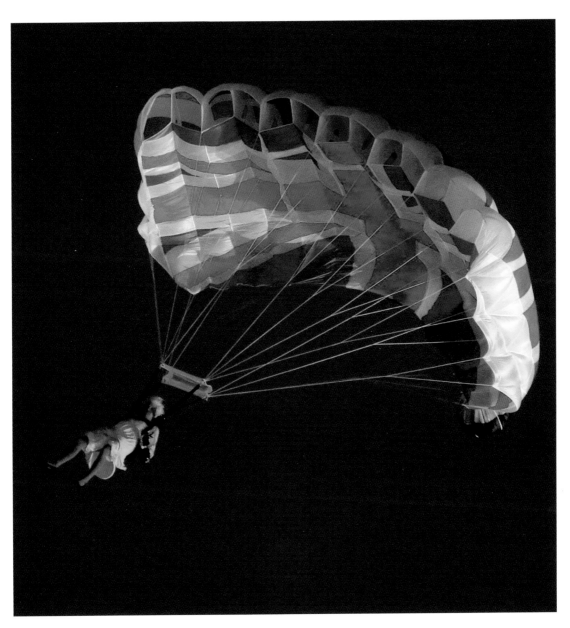

The Queen's stunt double parachutes into the Olympic Stadium.

The Queen formally opens the London Olympics on July 27, 2012.

An event by a republican pressure group attracted only 60 people, and chants of "Lizzie, Lizzie, Lizzie, Out, Out, Out" were drowned out by "God Save the Queen".

Sir David Attenborough, who was born a couple of weeks after the Queen, has joked that people often acquire "national treasure" status because they have been around such a long time. It is true that the Queen's longevity contributed to her appeal. She was on the throne throughout the lives of the majority of her subjects and as the years elapsed between past tawdry events and the later images of her indefatigable dutifulness, there was a growing appreciation of her as a comforting presence. Through financial meltdown and political crisis, she remained constant, calm and rarely emotional – unless one of her horses was winning. She ploughed on with public appearances, private audiences and official briefings.

It is easier for a nation to feel well disposed towards a happy family, and as time passed hers looked so much happier. Camilla Parker Bowles, once so unpopular that she was pelted with rolls in a supermarket, was not only brought into the fold but has won public acceptance and is now Queen Consort. More than that: with her down-to-earth humour and light touch, she proves popular when she carries out her royal duties.

Prince William went a step farther and married into the middle class. Kate Middleton's parents, former British Airways employees, run a mail-order party business and she has ancestors who were Geordie coalminers. Their wedding in 2011 saw a million people on the streets of London and hundreds of millions watching worldwide. It was a feelgood event at a time when the country had been mired in the longest period of austerity in living memory.

The Queen looks out from a carriage window at Edinburgh's Waverley Station, after boarding a steam train to inaugurate the £294 million Scottish Borders Railway, on September 9, 2015 – the day she became Britain's longest-reigning monarch.

A packed Mall during the Queen's Diamond Jubilee on June 5, 2012.

Prince Philip, the Queen, the Duchess of Cornwall and the Duchess of Cambridge on board the Spirit of Chartwell *on a very wet day at the Diamond Jubilee pageant on the Thames.*

*The Duchess of Cambridge and the Queen watch a children's sports
event in Nottingham during the Diamond Jubilee year.*

George, Charlotte and Louis have completed the picture of a fully functional family that has rediscovered its mojo and is closer to the rest of the population than before. George, born to live in a palace, spends many weekends with his mother's parents who have proved hands-on grandparents in a way that a future king has probably never experienced before.

The maturing of Prince Harry during his late twenties, when he showed humour and much of his mother's humanity on tours and in charity work, helped him for a time to become a more popular member of the clan. His marriage in 2018 to a mixed-race, and divorced, American actress, Meghan Markle, similarly had the effect of refreshing the brand, even if the new gilt was tarnished by the Sussexes' move to California and the subsequent public rift with the family. Its impact on the future of a more slimline monarchy itself, however, is likely to be limited.

The royal family plots its long-term strategy carefully and has benefited in recent decades from the professionalisation of its household. Though the family is traditionally comfortable surrounded by aristocrats, the Queen's key advisers during the years of transformation were her private secretary, Sir Christopher (now Lord) Geidt, and his predecessor Lord Janvrin, both former diplomats.

The household has embraced social media but has not lost its ability to pull off the best pageantry in the world. There were the two royal weddings (William and Kate's in 2011 and Harry and Meghan's in 2018) and, in 2012, the Diamond Jubilee weekend. This extravaganza concluded with a service at St Paul's Cathedral and a balcony appearance at the palace that featured only six family members: the Queen, the Prince of Wales, the Duchess of Cornwall, the Duke and Duchess of Cambridge and Prince Harry. The tableau sent a message that here was a streamlined unit focused on keeping the family business going.

Earlier a 1,000-strong flotilla processed down the Thames on a miserably wet day when onlookers and monarch were united in a soggy, dogged desire to celebrate the glorious nuttiness of being British. At the celebratory concert Madness sang "Our house, in the middle of one's street" from the roof of Buckingham Palace. Britain felt like one nation.

Even if that mood had changed somewhat by 2022, the Queen's Platinum Jubilee nevertheless united the country once more. While the Sussexes may have faded from the picture, the Cambridges' children were becoming gradually more central to it (even if Prince Louis's aggrieved reaction to the noise of the RAF's flypast suggested that he had yet to come to terms with that). The Queen knew her legacy was secure.

When the Queen became the UK's longest-reigning monarch she was less keen to celebrate. The moment arrived on the afternoon of Wednesday, September 9, 2015, when she had been on the throne for 23,226 days, 16 hours and 23 minutes, passing Queen Victoria's record. For various reasons, not least that her accession was bound up with the death of her father, she was reluctant to make any fuss, but eventually agreed to open the Borders Railway that day.

Standing next to Scotland's first minister, Nicola Sturgeon, after journeying by steam train from Edinburgh to Tweedbank, the Queen alluded briefly to her new place in the history books. "Many, including you, first minister, have also kindly noted another significance attaching to today, although it is not one to which I have ever aspired. Inevitably, a long life can pass by many milestones; my own is no exception. But I thank you all, and the many others at home and overseas, for your touching messages of great kindness."

Prince William chauffeurs his bride from the palace after their wedding reception on April 29, 2011.

Left: Prince Charles and the Duchess of Cornwall take part, with gusto, in a parachute game at a youth festival in Guernsey, July 2012. Right: The RAF's Red Arrows execute a flypast for the Diamond Jubilee.

*Prince George accompanied his parents, the Duke and Duchess of Cambridge,
on a trip to Canada in 2016.*

JUST GRANNY

by Damian Whitworth

To the world she was the Queen, but to her eight grandchildren she was "Granny". Prince William once explained the reality of growing up as a grandson of the most famous woman in the world. "She's my grandmother to me first and then she's the Queen."

This was demonstrated most clearly in the hours after the death of his mother, Diana, Princess of Wales, in 1997. The Queen was widely criticised when she did not return from Balmoral to London where large crowds were mourning. On this occasion, however, her instincts as a grandmother trumped her sense of duty as Queen. Her first priority was to stay with William and Harry in Scotland and help them grieve in private.

Long before then, William had developed a close bond with his grandmother, whose weekend home was a short walk from his school. Most weekends during his years at Eton he would walk across the river to spend time at Windsor Castle with "Granny". He and Harry both shouted, "Go, Granny!" during the opening ceremony of the 2012 Olympics when a stunt appeared to show Her Majesty parachuting out of a helicopter with Daniel Craig's James Bond.

After his wedding in 2011, Prince William offered a fascinating insight into how the Queen could cut through royal pomp to ensure he and his intended bride were not swamped by tradition. Once William had announced his engagement to Kate Middleton, palace bureaucracy swung into action on a scale that alarmed the prince.

"I was given this official list of 777 names – dignitaries, governors, all sorts of people – and not one person I knew," he recalled. "They said: 'These are the people we should invite.' I looked at it in absolute horror and said: 'I think we should start again.'

"I rang [the Queen] up the next day and said: 'Do we need to be doing this?' And she said: 'No. Start with your friends first and then go from there.' And she told me to bin the list. She made the point that there are certain times when you have to strike the right balance. And it's advice like that which is really key, when you know that she's seen and done it before."

The Queen's grandchildren are Prince William and Prince Harry, sons of the Prince of Wales; Peter Phillips and Zara Tindall, the children of the Princess Royal; Princess Beatrice and Princess Eugenie, the daughters of the Duke of York; Lady Louise Windsor and James, Viscount Severn, the offspring of the Earl of Wessex.

There are also 12 great-grandchildren: Prince George, Princess Charlotte and Prince Louis; Archie and Lilibet Mountbatten-Windsor; Savannah and Isla Phillips; Mia, Lena and Lucas Tindall; August Brooksbank, the son of Princess Eugenie; and Sienna Mozzi, the daughter of Princess Beatrice. The Queen particularly enjoyed her annual pre-Christmas lunch at Buckingham Palace, which provides an opportunity to get together as much of the extended family as possible.

The Queen was also known as "Granny" to Prince George. That became clear after Charlotte's christening, when William was heard telling him "we can go back to Granny's". That was Sandringham, the main house on the estate where they also live, in Anmer Hall.

The Duke of York once suggested that the Queen was more comfortable as a grandmother than she was a mother, which was hardly surprising given that she was a young woman when she had to juggle motherhood with monarchy.

"She's been a fantastic grandmother to Beatrice and Eugenie and probably revels in that more than being a mother, to some extent. Always interested and concerned for what the girls are up to," Prince Andrew said at the time of her Diamond Jubilee.

The grandchildren...

Peter Phillips
*(son of the
Princess Royal)*

Zara Tindall
*(daughter of the
Princess Royal)*

Prince William
*(son of the
Prince of Wales)*

Prince Harry
*(son of the
Prince of Wales)*

Princess Beatrice
*(daughter of the
Duke of York)*

Princess Eugenie
*(daughter of the
Duke of York)*

Lady Louise Windsor
*(daughter of the
Earl of Wessex)*

James, Viscount Severn
*(son of the
Earl of Wessex)*

Eugenie described a grandmother who "lit up" around her grandchildren. She would take them raspberry picking when Eugenie was young and listened to her stories of life at Newcastle University, taking an interest in what essays she was writing.

In recent years the Queen was very close to her youngest grandchildren, the children of the Earl of Wessex, who decided against giving them the titles of prince and princess. The family live at Bagshot Park, a short drive from Windsor, where the children often went riding with their grandmother.

As a young girl, Lady Louise, now in her late teens, bore a striking physical resemblance to her grandmother at the same age, and she spent time talking horses with the Queen at the Royal Mews at Windsor where her pony was stabled.

The Queen liked nothing more than to attend events where she had a role as both grandmother and Queen. At William's passing-out parade at Sandhurst in 2006 she managed to make her grandson smile as she inspected the solemn-faced new officers in her role as commander-in-chief of the armed forces. William said that his grandmother liked to laugh about things that went wrong at formal events. "The Queen has seen so many parades or performances, when there's a small slip-up it tickles her humour."

He also said, bearing in mind that he will one day sit on the throne, that she was a constant source of counsel. "There's no question you can ask, and no point you can raise, that she won't already know about – and have a better opinion about," he told the author Robert Hardman for his book *Our Queen*. "And for me particularly, being the young bloke coming through, being able to talk to my grandmother, ask her questions and know that there's sound advice coming back is very reassuring."

After going to see victims of the Australian floods and New Zealand earthquake in 2011 William received a note from the Queen congratulating him on the way he represented her. "When you get a letter from her or a bit of praise, it goes a long, long way, more so than anyone else saying, 'Well done' to you. There's such gravitas behind those words."

She saw her grandchildren make mistakes, but their indiscretions came with the added complication that they were often splashed across newspapers: Harry in a Nazi uniform, smoking cannabis or playing strip poker in Las Vegas; William landing his helicopter in the back garden of Kate's parents' home.

One of the few occasions when Buckingham Palace made it clear that the monarch disapproved of a grandchild's behaviour was when Peter Phillips sold the photographs of his wedding at Windsor Castle to *Hello!* magazine. And there were raised eyebrows when his sister, Zara, and her husband, Mike Tindall, appeared in the same magazine with their daughter Mia.

There is no doubt that in private the Queen could be clear and forthright when she needed to be. William may have found Granny was relaxed about the wedding guest list but when he started weighing up which military uniform he would wear on the day, she told him there was no question he should wear his Irish Guards uniform. "I was given a categorical, 'No, you'll wear this.' So you don't always get what you want, put it that way."

Prince William can't help smiling at his grandmother during his passing-out parade at Sandhurst, 2006.

Harry with his grandmother after Prince Charles's wedding to Camilla Parker Bowles, 2005.

The Queen has always shared a passion for horses with her grandchildren, especially Zara Tindall, pictured here at the Cheltenham Gold Cup race meeting in March 2003.

The Queen with Princess Eugenie at the traditional Royal Maundy Service at St George's Chapel, 2019.

THE FUTURE:
GEORGE, CHARLOTTE & LOUIS

by Valentine Low

It is a close call as to which has the greater power to increase the popularity of the monarchy: a royal wedding or a royal birth. However, there was no doubt that the arrival of Prince George in 2013 was yet another boost for the royal family's public standing. Even the most curmudgeonly republicans silenced their complaints for a day.

Prince George was more than just a bonny baby, however. His birth heralded something far more important: it signified lineage and longevity. The point was brought home in fairly unsubtle style at George's christening in October of that year when an official photograph was released showing, for the first time since 1894, four generations of the royal family gathered together: the Queen, the Prince of Wales, the Duke of Cambridge and Prince George. The line of succession was, barring some terrible misfortune, safe for many decades to come.

The Queen, of course, was delighted at the birth of the third in line to the throne (her third great-grandchild). Two days after George was born, she took the rare step of driving to Kensington Palace to meet the new addition. Usually, visitors came to see her.

Prince George was an immediate international superstar. He was inundated with presents from all over the world, and he accompanied his parents to Australia and New Zealand the following year. At home, he has been a regular visitor to Buckingham Palace, where the duchess started taking him for weekly swimming lessons before he turned one – a habit that must have strengthened his relationship with his great-grandmother. He even went there on his first birthday, the same day that the Queen made a point of attending his birthday party at Kensington Palace.

As the third in line to the throne, Prince George *immediately became an international superstar.*

If the birth of Princess Charlotte in 2015 – in and out of the Lindo Wing at St Mary's Hospital in a day – was surrounded by marginally less excitement, as the line of succession had been secured, there was still plenty of fanfare, from gun salutes to the equally traditional vigil outside the hospital by foreign news crews.

By then, the Cambridges had moved into Anmer Hall on the Sandringham Estate, which could only have pleased the Queen, as it allowed her the opportunity to see George and Charlotte more frequently, and with far less public scrutiny, than she did in London. The arrival of Prince Louis of Cambridge in 2018 completed the family, even as the duke and duchess began to take on a larger and more prominent share of royal duties.

Then within a few years, Prince George started to be seen with his parents as they performed those duties, for instance attending the final of the European football championship at Wembley in 2021. The result, as England lost to Italy, no doubt disappointed him – although he may have to get used to that – but for the monarchy his identification with the nation's hopes was another milestone reached. The cycle had begun anew, and the future secured once more.

Left: The birth of Princess Charlotte on May 2, 2015.
Right: The birth of Prince Louis on April 23, 2018.

The Duke and Duchess of Cambridge with their three children,
George, Charlotte and Louis, at the Trooping the Colour ceremony, 2019.

~ A Prince's Repose ~

A Christian funeral is a ceremony to honour the departed and seek solace for their soul. It also has a wider significance: to honour the person interred, recall their achievements in life and bring together in comfort and reverence those to whom he or she was closest. All these elements will mark the funeral today in St George's Chapel, Windsor, of the Duke of Edinburgh. It will not be a state funeral, partly because of his own wish and partly because of the restrictions imposed by the coronavirus. But it will still be the most poignant event for the Queen in her long reign. It will bring to an end a royal partnership that has brought stability and continuity to the United Kingdom for almost all the postwar era. And it heralds the transition to a new concept of monarchy that will, in future, be very different from what Prince Philip knew.

The symbolism of today's events has been planned in meticulous detail. Those attending, limited to no more than 30 in accordance with current restrictions affecting every funeral in the country, have been invited because of warm family ties and because of their personal friendship with the prince. Neither the prime minister nor any other political dignitary will be present. Civic leaders have already expressed, often eloquently, the nation's debt to Prince Philip over the past week of official mourning. It has been a difficult decision for the Queen to choose which duke, princess, cousin and grandchild to include and which will have to watch the ceremonies, like millions of Britons and people around the world, on television. But three of the mourners are of particular significance: the princes from Germany who are part of Prince Philip's extended family there and elsewhere in continental Europe.

Although himself a distant descendant of Queen Victoria, Prince Philip was not a native Briton. He adopted this country, and on his marriage dedicated his life to serving it as wholeheartedly as he had served during the war in the Royal Navy. None of his older sisters, married to Germans, was invited to his wedding: in 1947 popular sentiment was still raw. But the prince, whose early schooling was in Germany and who remained close to his German relatives throughout his life, brought a wider international perspective to the monarchy. He travelled to almost every country in the world, and with the Queen was a vigorous champion of the Commonwealth. His death has been mourned there to a degree that many younger Britons may not have realised: in Canada, Australia and New Zealand, and also in the Caribbean, the south Pacific and remote British overseas territories, he was seen as a figure who knew and understood their peoples even if official London seemed increasingly distant.

Much has been made of the naval and military symbols and personnel who will escort the coffin to the chapel, together with the choice of the "Eternal Father" hymn invoking those at sea (though not to be sung by the congregation, in keeping, again, with restrictions). The navy was where Prince Philip's heart lay. The Land Rover that he himself designed to bear his coffin represents his own intense interest in engineering and technology. More surprising, perhaps, is the decision that military uniforms are not to be worn. This partly reflects the prince's wish for a pared-down ceremony without flamboyance or fuss. It is also an appropriate way to avoid embarrassing Prince Harry, who is no longer entitled to wear a uniform.

The public will naturally look for signs of any reconciliation between Prince Harry and his elder brother, the Duke of Cambridge, after the frosty public comments made about him in Prince Harry's television interview. In walking behind the coffin, the brothers will be diplomatically separated by their cousin, Peter Phillips.

The issue is symbolic now of the challenge facing not only the Queen but increasingly the Prince of Wales, who will inevitably take over more of the monarch's official duties. Questions abound. How should the monarchy adapt to new times and changed expectations? To what extent do the foibles and antics of the wider royal family damage the monarchy's purpose? Would a more narrow focus allow younger princes and princesses to escape the attention and also the censure they have incurred? Indeed, should they have titles at all if not close to the throne?

As Prince Charles has clearly understood, and as shown by the number of complaints the BBC received over what was seen as excessive coverage, a younger generation no longer has the same interest in the royal family or deference to its constitutional role. Prince Philip, in his younger days, was central to efforts to modernise royal protocol, define royal duties, cut free from the flummery that seemed to envelop the institution, and keep the monarchy in tune with contemporary social attitudes. His achievement, in the face of much opposition, was significant and accounts largely for the monarchy's enduring popularity.

But times and views have changed. It is only 19 years since there was an outpouring of popular emotion and ceremonial pomp that marked the funeral of the Queen Mother. Those emotions have given way sometimes to indifference and occasionally to exasperation. Public comment on Prince Andrew has been personal and hostile; coverage of the monarchy has tended to focus now on cost and privilege. The foibles and rivalries that once entertained many Britons, and especially European tabloids, are seen as something more destructive that could tear apart a family once so united for its balcony appearances.

Prince Philip witnessed a long decline in the economic power, global influence and moral authority of the country he had made his own. He and the Queen have presided over the transformation of empire to

Commonwealth. More recently, there has been fierce public controversy over how the legacy of empire should be assessed. Britain, however, even when no longer joined with its former partners in the European Union, remains a country of immense achievement, promise and influence. And the monarchy remains central to the concept of nationhood, even if the unity of the United Kingdom may now be called into question. Those proposing its abolition have yet to offer an alternative that commands popular support and the backing of a long history and heritage.

The Duke of Edinburgh's death may seem to many to mark the closure of an age. In truth, it is part of an ever-changing institution that is defined as much by its principal players as by the expectations of those it serves. Prince Philip, for all the stories that have emerged of his contrariness and occasional hauteur, was a man of moral strength and humane vision. He led his family and influenced its actions in a way that even the Queen was happy to acknowledge and salute. He will be laid to rest today with the thanks of a nation for a life well lived and a purpose well served.

The Times, April 17, 2021

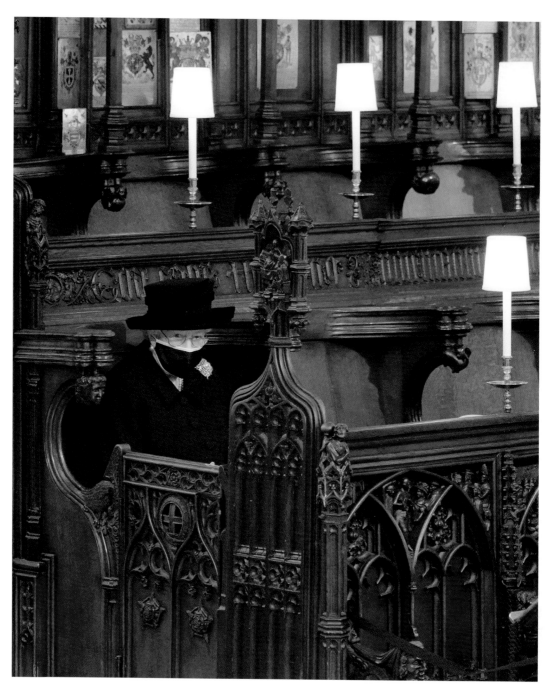

The Queen sits alone at Prince Philip's funeral, which took place on April 17, 2021, amid the restrictions set during the coronavirus pandemic.

Prince Philip, Duke of Edinburgh: June 10, 1921, to April 9, 2021.

AFTER PHILIP

by Matthew Dennison

At Buckingham Palace, scaffolding has obscured the grand staircase for much of the past two years. Largely out of action were the famous curving stairs, with their sweep of gilded balustrade, out of sight the soaring portraits of William IV and Queen Adelaide at the stairs' summit.

Typically, every year, the state apartments dazzle an admiring public. At present, much of the palace looks more like a building site; even rooms not subject to repairs have been repurposed as (admittedly grand) storage spaces. The programme of upgrading services throughout the palace – due for completion in 2027 – is not a glamorous one; wall pipes are being replaced and new water tanks installed; leaking roofs have been fixed, including re-roofing the picture gallery; a new energy centre is being built.

Even the royal family's private apartments, including the Queen's, have been steadily licked into shape, a process made easier by the pandemic, which led to the Queen and her children vacating the capital's smartest office spaces to work from home in the country. In the Queen's case, this meant Windsor Castle. She retreated to Windsor in March 2020, to be shortly joined by Prince Philip, from his retirement home of Wood Farm on the Sandringham estate. There the couple lived with a reduced household of Covid-safe attendants affectionately labelled "HMS Bubble".

None of the Queen's ladies-in-waiting – that handful of women who accompanied her on engagements and managed her correspondence, including, from 2017, two members of the Queen Mother's extended family, Susan Rhodes and Lady Elizabeth Leeming – was at the Queen's side continually throughout lockdown; the ladies-in-waiting also worked mostly from home. In the spring of 2022, offices in Buckingham Palace returned to something approaching normality (as did the Grand Staircase). Despite the scaffolding and disruption elsewhere, insiders insisted that it was still a working palace.

The message from palace staff was unequivocal: for Team Royal, it was business as usual. As always, the directive was the Queen's. Her husband's death deprived her of the last of her closest family confidants, following the deaths of her sister, her mother and her cousin, Margaret Rhodes. But the Queen was not a sentimental woman. Her first mistress of the robes once described her as "very practical", and her sanctioning of wide-ranging palace repairs was also typical of her concern for the monarchy's future smooth running.

If it was business as usual for the palace, the same applied to its nonagenarian figurehead. Royal employees pointed out that the Queen's enjoyment of "getting out and about and meeting people" remained undimmed. One also reminded me of the promise of lifelong service she made in Cape Town in 1947. For the Queen, then, business as usual meant going out and doing her duty, dressed in her customary bright colour-block outfits of coat and matching hat and with a smile on her face. As her former Archbishop of Canterbury Robert Runcie noted in the 1990s, "With her, duty comes first, even above family problems."

In the wake of the death of the Duke of Edinburgh, it was an impressive show of resilience and dedication. At Windsor, in the final weeks of the duke's life, the couple's world shrank. Reunited by the pandemic, for a year they were able to share the sort of leisurely togetherness other elderly couples enjoy, walking in the castle's private gardens and dining together without interruptions or the inevitable separations of busy public lives; they managed a last, short return to Wood Farm at the end of the summer.

After the duke's discharge from hospital, there was less time outside and formal meal times were abandoned. Philip slept a lot during the day, his appetite depleted, his mobility limited, although he continued to receive and write letters and stay in touch with close friends and family by telephone. The Queen understood the implications of his determination not to return to hospital. Although his death, on April 9, 2021, was peaceful and not unexpected, inevitably it shook the spouse who had fallen in love with her handsome, square-jawed prince at the age of 13. Prince Edward described his mother soon afterwards as "bearing up".

Whatever her unhappiness, it was almost certainly the Queen's wishes that restricted royal mourning for her beloved husband to two weeks, ending after his funeral, although the Palace explained it at the time as a family decision. Nothing in her behaviour afterwards suggested a monarch keen on protracted grieving in public. Perhaps she appeared unusually sombre at the state opening of parliament in May 2021, the first ceremonial duty of her widowhood. Commentators who suggested the Queen had chosen to wear traditional half-mourning as a mark of her sadness overlooked her choice of the same flower-print frock she had previously worn on a happier occasion, for photographs released to mark Prince Philip's 99th birthday.

Nor did thoughts of Philip explain her absence from the first day of Royal Ascot. Instead, in her capacity as head of the Commonwealth and Queen of Australia, the Queen was at work, entertaining Australia's prime minister, Scott Morrison. She wore another brightly coloured frock and, in a characteristic diplomatic pleasantry, the large brooch of white and yellow diamonds, in the shape of Australia's national wattle flower, which Australians had presented to her on her first visit to the country in 1954. At the end of the week, she was present for the final day's racing at Ascot. Her decision to dispense with traditional black-bordered writing paper – instead, on the Queen's stationery, her crest appeared in black rather than red – also pointed to a desire to limit external signs of grief.

Indeed, some observed how cheerful she seemed when out and about. Perhaps this was to be expected after so many months of confinement; after all, at the time of the duke's death, many aspects of life had yet to open up. She was said to be spending her time in those early weeks tuning in to the BBC police drama *Line of Duty*, discussing the plot with one of her closest aides, Vice-Admiral Sir Tony Johnstone-Burt. There was additional sadness in May when a puppy given to her by the Duke of York died (she was reportedly given another on June 10, the centenary of Prince Philip's birth). Perhaps it was little wonder she appeared so pleased to have resumed a busy schedule of public engagements.

For her return to full-time royal engagements the Queen gathered around her a small team of trusted intimates. As throughout lockdown, she remained in regular contact with members of her immediate family. Of her four children, Prince Andrew lived the closest, at Royal Lodge in Windsor Great Park, where the Queen spent much of her childhood. Eleven miles away were Prince Edward and his wife, Sophie, with whom the Queen shared a notably warm relationship, both unassuming, modest women and linked by interests including a fondness for military history.

In the Sussexes' absence, Princess Eugenie and her husband, Jack Brooksbank, moved into Frogmore Cottage, which gave the Queen a much-loved granddaughter within easy striking distance. In addition, the Queen came to rely on the support of members of her household, including the lady-in-waiting who accompanied her to Prince Philip's funeral and Royal Ascot and her senior dresser. The first was 82-year-old Lady Susan Hussey, since 1996 Baroness Hussey, the second Angela Kelly.

In 2020 Hussey celebrated 60 years as a lady-in-waiting; her discretion, tact and humour have endeared her to generations of royals, including her godson, the Duke of Cambridge. In 2013 she received the Queen's highest mark of favour, when she was appointed Dame Grand Cross of the Royal Victorian Order, an honour more usually reserved for members of the Queen's family (other recipients include the Princess Royal, Princess Alexandra, the Countess of Wessex, the Duchess of Cornwall and the Duchess of Cambridge).

Kelly is a lively Liverpudlian divorcée in her late sixties and was unashamedly devoted to the Queen. At intervals her meteoric career rise inspired sniping within palace walls. Different in background, outlook and temperament, both women earned and repaid the Queen's trust. Hussey shared a lifetime of memories with her royal employer, beginning with the birth of Prince Andrew. A widow since 2006, she could provide sympathetic companionable understanding.

The Queen surrounded herself with close aides after Prince Philip's death. She is pictured here with one of the closest, Vice-Admiral Sir Tony Johnstone-Burt.

After the Duke of Edinburgh's death, the Queen threw herself straight back into her royal duties, here entertaining Australia's prime minister Scott Morrison.

Lady Hussey, lady-in-waiting, was a great support to the Queen.

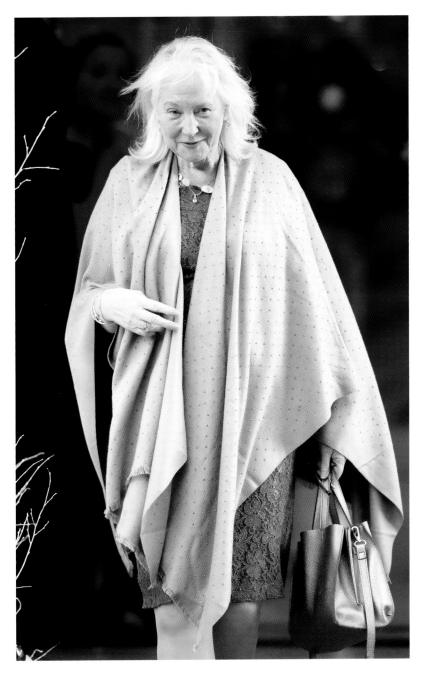

The Queen also came to rely on the support of Angela Kelly, her senior dresser.

That the Queen chose wisely is obvious to anyone who witnessed her later engagements. At first, a view was widespread that the Duke of Edinburgh's death would inevitably lead to a scaling back in the Queen's public life as she grappled with her grief. There were even suggestions that, like Queen Victoria, she planned to retreat to Balmoral and the privacy of the Highlands.

The Queen did indeed go to Scotland. Holyrood Week has long been a fixture in the royal diary and one the half-Scottish Queen looked forward to keenly. Usually she held investitures and garden parties at her Edinburgh palace, but not in 2021, on account of Covid restrictions. Instead, the Queen went out and about. The Duke of Cambridge accompanied her on a visit to a soft drinks factory in Cumbernauld; two days later, with the Princess Royal, she visited a community nature reserve in Glasgow. In Edinburgh, again accompanied by her daughter, the Queen was given two young trees to plant as part of a Platinum Jubilee conservation initiative, the Queen's Green Canopy. It was all a far cry from grieving at Balmoral.

Like those of many of her subjects in post-Covid Britain, the Queen's was a hybrid working life. Adept at Zoom, unlike her late husband, she continued to carry out virtual engagements. New Ghanaian, Iranian, Israeli and Chinese ambassadors, for instance, were received virtually. The Queen spoke to leaders of the Queen's Commonwealth Trust, an initiative founded in her name in 2018 to raise funds for young people in the Commonwealth. For a sovereign in her tenth decade who no longer undertook long-haul travel but remained head of a Commonwealth of more than 50 nations, the altered working practices of the pandemic offered an unexpected boon: the possibility of continuing her overseas work from home.

Although those in charge of the royal diary had been on standby for restart "for a while", the Queen's hybrid public life continued in this vein for some time. Resignedly – or perhaps it was simply a reflection of the Queen's unfussy pragmatism – everyone concerned appeared quite happy with this. The Queen continued to deal with her governors-general virtually. Red boxes of state papers arrived at Windsor Castle daily; the business of state continued.

Only in the last few months of her life did this rhythm begin to change. In July 2022, Prince Charles stood in for her at the opening of the Commonwealth Games. A week later, her traditional welcome at her summer retreat of Balmoral was held in private. It was apparent that she had become more frail, a turn of events underscored by her missing the Braemar Gathering at the Highland Games in early September. Yet the Queen was determined to "see off her 14th prime minister and welcome her 15th", as Boris Johnson later told the House of Commons. The following evening came the first sign that anything was amiss, when the Privy Council meeting convened to hear Liz Truss take her oath of office was cancelled.

Undoubtedly, the Queen's life since Prince Philip's death lacked the tranquillity of their final shared months. Although she reportedly visited the Duke of Sussex after his arrival in the UK in July 2021 for the unveiling of a memorial to Diana, Princess of Wales, rifts within the royal family persisted, and were described by Prince Edward as "difficult". There could be little doubt, however, that her return to public life, supported by her family and members of her inner circle, was a cause for pleasure for the elderly sovereign. The Queen told listeners to her Easter broadcast in 2020, "Dark as death can be... light and life are greater." All the evidence suggests she meant it.

END
OF A REIGN

~ Queen Elizabeth II dies ~

Her Majesty the Queen, the longest-reigning monarch this country has known, has died peacefully at Balmoral.

As messages of sympathy arrived from around the world the new King, who will reign as Charles III, led the tributes to his "beloved mother" as he spoke of the "greatest sadness" for his family.

Charles spoke of his grief and the "respect and deep affection" in which the Queen was "so widely held".

His words came soon after Buckingham Palace confirmed that Elizabeth II, 96, who served as head of state for more than 70 years, died peacefully yesterday afternoon.

Charles said in a written statement: "The death of my beloved Mother, Her Majesty The Queen, is a moment of the greatest sadness for me and all members of my family.

"We mourn profoundly the passing of a cherished Sovereign and a much-loved Mother.

"I know her loss will be deeply felt throughout the country, the Realms and the Commonwealth, and by countless people around the world.

"During this period of mourning and change, my family and I will be comforted and sustained by our knowledge of the respect and deep affection in which The Queen was so widely held."

Addressing the nation from Downing Street, Liz Truss announced Charles's new title. The prime minister said: "Today the crown passes, as it has done for more than 1,000 years, to our new monarch, to our new head of state, His Majesty King Charles III."

The palace announcement, which came at 6.30pm, said: "The Queen died peacefully at Balmoral this afternoon.

"The King and The Queen Consort will remain at Balmoral this evening and will return to London tomorrow."

It followed hours of rising concern about the Queen after the Palace said at 12.30pm that doctors were "concerned for Her Majesty's health".

As members of her family, including all four of her children and Prince William, now known as the Duke of Cornwall and Cambridge, started gathering at Balmoral, it became clear that the Queen's life was drawing to a close.

Charles will formally be proclaimed as the new sovereign at St James's Palace tomorrow. He is expected to give a televised address to the nation this evening at 6pm.

The Queen, who acceded to the throne on February 6, 1952, upon the death of her father, George VI, will be given a state funeral at Westminster Abbey, the first state funeral since that of Sir Winston Churchill in 1965.

It will follow a lying in state at Westminster Hall, during which members of the public will have the opportunity to pay their respects. Books of condolence will be opened at St James's Palace, the Queen's Gallery, next to Buckingham Palace, Windsor Castle, Holyroodhouse in Edinburgh, Balmoral and Sandringham.

The Queen's death marks the passing of the only sovereign most people in Britain have known.

She served her country through war, peace, social upheaval and technological revolution, a symbol of continuity and steadfast devotion to duty while the world changed around her.

History will deliver its verdict in the fullness of time but it is hard to conceive of her being remembered as anything other than one of the greatest monarchs in our history, a figure to rank alongside her namesake Elizabeth I and Queen Victoria.

Although her death is the closing of a chapter for these islands, the end of the modern Elizabethan era, it will also be mourned around the world. She was head of state for 14 other nations, from Canada and Australia to the tiny Pacific island of Tuvalu.

She broke records, including becoming the world's oldest reigning monarch, the longest-reigning of her time and the most travelled. In September 2015 she passed Victoria's record for the longest reign this country has known. Yet the numbers do not say how, by her modesty, her self-sacrifice, her commitment and her seriousness of purpose, she became a revered figure around the world.

She was not born to be Queen. As the daughter of the Duke of York, the second son of George V, she was destined for a life of relative royal obscurity until her uncle, Edward VIII, abdicated and her father became George VI.

Elizabeth became Queen before she expected to, after her father died

of lung cancer at the age of 56 while she was on tour in Kenya. She was 25 and, although already a mother of two, was young enough to be embraced in those post-war years as a symbol of youth, promise and a brighter future.

Britain underwent vast social change during her reign. But while the Queen seemed a symbol of constancy, her great achievement was to change while appearing to remain the same. The monarch who had carried on working – unquestioning, uncomplaining – long past the age of retirement was recognisably the same woman, with the same values, who on her 21st birthday declared that "my whole life, whether it be long or short, shall be devoted to your service"

But times had changed, and so had she. The Queen who welcomed Camilla into the royal family after the bitterness of the Diana years, who gave her blessing to the James Bond stunt for the opening ceremony of the London Olympics, was a very different creature from the one who waved a white-gloved hand at the crowds on her first great Commonwealth tour.

More recently, when the monarchy had been rocked by the departure of the Duke and Duchess of Sussex and the scandal over the Duke of York, she showed she could still provide leadership, giving a televised address during the coronavirus pandemic. After the death of the Duke of Edinburgh, her husband of 73 years, in April last year she threw herself back into royal duties with an energy and a commitment that belied her age.

Her story is, in a sense, our story. Now she is dead, the mourning begins; a mourning not just about grief, but public reflection, as we consider who we are and what we have become.

Before her funeral at Westminster Abbey in ten days her body will be taken to Westminster Hall to lie in state, so that people may pay their respects. When the Queen Mother died, thousands of mourners waited for up to six hours to see her.

There will be queues.

The Times, September 9, 2022

QUEEN ELIZABETH II
OBITUARY

When the Queen became this country's longest-serving monarch, the humility with which she acknowledged the passing of that historic moment reflected the same selfless dedication with which she once promised to serve her people. Some 68 years separated the pledge she made in Cape Town on her 21st birthday and the modest speech that she made on passing Queen Victoria's record in September 2015, but even if the empire to which she devoted herself no longer exists, the values she spoke of then were the values to which she still held true a lifetime later. "My whole life," she said, in that resonant passage that captured imaginations worldwide in 1947, "whether it be long or short, shall be devoted to your service."

It was, in the event, a long life, one that both straddled history and made history. Born at the time of the General Strike, she acceded to the throne at a time when members of the royal family were still treated with a reverence that seems alien today. By the time she died, she had lived through an era of vast social, material and technological change, from a period when few people had television sets to the age of the internet.

She was a symbol, but what she symbolised changed over the years. At the beginning of her reign, her youth and beauty – set against the austerity and uncertainty of the postwar years – were seized on as an emblem of hope, a harbinger of a new Elizabethan age. If along the way she was regarded by some as a totem of all that was wrong with a class-ridden society, by her later years she came to stand for those old-fashioned virtues that are in such short supply these days: service, duty, modesty, self-sacrifice and hard work.

Yet it is important to remember that beneath the crown there was also a woman, a wife, a mother. She had to cope with the early death of her father and, later, the indignity of unsparing public scrutiny as the marriages of three of her children collapsed. Too frequently the human side of her character – her talent for mimicry, her sense of fun, the way she came to life when she was watching her racehorses in action – was overlooked as a nation concentrated instead on the cipher it wanted to see. That oversight may have been partly her own work, as she spent her life presenting a public image suitable for the head of state. However, it was one of the many remarkable aspects of her that, unlike most, she became more relaxed and open to new suggestions as she grew older: who would have believed that the Queen we once knew would have agreed to take part in a stunt with James Bond for the opening of the London 2012 Olympics?

Above all, she was the woman who saved the monarchy in this country. That is not to say that without her we would have had a republic by now, or that the monarchy did not endure some troubled times during her reign when the unpopularity of some of its members led critics to question its very future, but it is thanks to her dedication and seriousness of purpose that an institution that has at times seemed outdated and out of keeping with the values of contemporary society still has a relevance and popularity today. She made a promise in Cape Town, and she was as good as her word.

The future Queen Elizabeth II was born in the early hours of April 21, 1926. She was the daughter of the Duchess of York, the 25-year-old wife of George V's second son, Albert. The birth took place at 17 Bruton Street, Mayfair, the home of her mother's parents, the Earl and Countess of Strathmore. It was a difficult delivery: the official bulletin referred to medical complications and "a certain line of treatment", a circumlocution which the newspapers of the day declined to translate. She was delivered, in other words, by caesarean section.

Although Elizabeth was not born to be queen – at that time, long before anyone had heard of Wallis Simpson, Albert's elder brother, David, was the heir to the throne and few saw any reason to doubt that the future Edward VIII would do his duty by providing the next generation of the royal family – her arrival prompted great excitement. Crowds gathered outside the house and the *Daily Sketch*, with perhaps less faith in the Prince of Wales than others, announced: "A possible Queen of England was born yesterday."

Among the first visitors to see the baby, named Elizabeth Alexandra Mary after her mother, great-grandmother and grandmother respectively, were the King and Queen. "Such a relief," wrote Queen Mary in her diary, noting that Elizabeth was "a little darling with lovely complexion & pretty fair hair".

In the ordered, upper-class existence of her parents, Elizabeth's world was the nursery, which was ruled over by the formidable figure of Clara Knight, who was known to her young charges as Allah. The distance between child and parent, which was common in aristocratic families of the time, was exacerbated by her parents' royal duties. When Elizabeth was only nine months old, the Duke and Duchess of York went on a tour of Australia and New Zealand that took them away for six months. "It quite broke me up," her mother wrote in her diary, recalling their parting. "The baby was so sweet, playing with the buttons on Bertie's uniform."

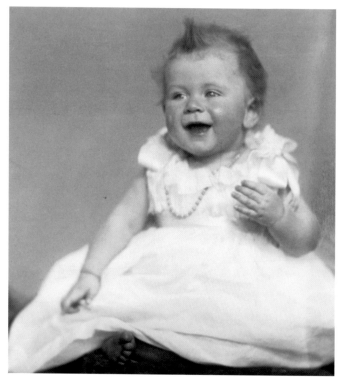

Childhood portrait of Queen Elizabeth II, as a baby in December 1926.

To judge by contemporary reports, Elizabeth was a solemn, self-contained child. Winston Churchill met her when he was invited to Balmoral in the autumn of 1928. "[She] is a character," the chancellor wrote to his wife, Clementine. "She had an air of authority and reflectiveness astonishing in an infant."

With her parents so often away, Elizabeth saw much of her grandparents, an arrangement that delighted them. During a three-month stay at Buckingham Palace, she would be brought down for tea every day with the King and Queen. "Here comes the Bambino!" the normally stiff Queen Mary would declare. According to some reports, the King used to play with his granddaughter in a way that he never did with his own children: he called her Lilibet, in imitation of her attempts to say her name. Her family called her Lilibet ever after. At Sandringham the King liked to have her sit next to him at breakfast and would take her round the Royal Stud to show her his favourite horses. It is more than likely that Elizabeth inherited her lifelong passion for horses from her grandfather, who gave the child her first pony, a shetland called Peggy, for her fourth birthday.

Outside the confines of palace life she was a celebrity. At the age of three, she was on the cover of *Time* magazine, an appearance that was credited with prompting a fashion for children being dressed in yellow instead of pink or blue after it was revealed that yellow was the predominant colour in both the royal nursery and Elizabeth's wardrobe. By the time she was four, and had a younger sister in the form of Margaret Rose, born at Glamis Castle, she had her own waxwork at Madame Tussauds – riding a pony (the second Tussauds waxwork to be made of her) – and a large slice of Antarctica had been named in her honour.

Even her father seemed swept up in the enthusiasm for the much-lauded young princess. Perhaps, he hinted one day in the early 1930s to the poet Osbert Sitwell, she was born for higher things. Comparing her to Queen Victoria, he gave Sitwell a meaningful look and said: "From the first moment of talking she showed so much character, that it was impossible not to wonder whether history would not repeat itself."

Princess Elizabeth and Princess Margaret with King George VI, while their mother chats to Lord Elphinstone during an inspection of the Royal Company of Archers at Holyrood Palace, Edinburgh, 1937.

As the girls grew up the Yorks – by now living at 145 Piccadilly, a large townhouse overlooking Green Park – came to be held in the popular imagination as a model family. They were royal, but sufficiently removed from the ceremonial of court life to represent an ideal to which Middle England could aspire. As Ben Pimlott, the historian, wrote, with the reserved, proud father, practical, child-centred mother, and well-groomed, well-mannered children, they were "a distillation of British wholesomeness".

For that contented family unit, happy with their place in the order of things – "us four", as Bertie called them – everything was to change in 1936. George V died on January 20, his end signalled by the famous medical bulletin from his doctor, Lord Dawson of Penn: "The King's life is moving peacefully towards its close."

When his body was brought to lie in state in Westminster Hall, the nine-year-old Elizabeth was allowed to stay up late to stand in front of the coffin as her father and three uncles stood at each corner.

The Abdication crisis that followed, when Edward VIII decided that he could not continue as King if he could not marry the twice-divorced Simpson, had such a devastating impact on the royal family that its repercussions are still felt today. It was suffered most immediately by Bertie, who did not want to be king, was rendered thoroughly miserable as the drama unfolded, and implored his elder brother to stay. When the decision was finally made Bertie, appalled by the burden facing him, broke down in tears on his mother's shoulder.

Elizabeth was now next in line to the throne. "When our father became King," Margaret recalled, "I said to her, 'Does that mean you're going to become Queen?' She replied, 'Yes, I suppose it does.' She didn't mention it again." According to her governess, Marion Crawford – "Crawfie" – Elizabeth was horrified to learn that they were to move to Buckingham Palace: "What – you mean for ever?"

Her father's coronation was on May 12, 1937, the day that had been reserved for the coronation of Edward VIII. In a diary written in the neat, rounded hand of the 11-year-old Elizabeth, she recorded all that happened that day, from the moment she leapt out of bed at 5am and crouched at the window with her nursemaid Margaret MacDonald – "Bobo" – looking at the crowds taking their places in the stands below, to the formal photographs at the end of the day, "in front of those awful lights". Westminster Abbey, she said, was "very, very wonderful". She wrote: "The arches and beams at the top were covered with a sort of haze of wonder as Papa was crowned, at least I thought so."

Elizabeth and Margaret were the last generation of the British royal family to be educated at home. There were French lessons with Antoinette de Bellaigue, dancing with Miss Vacani, drawing sessions and twice-weekly riding lessons; and, for Elizabeth, history with Sir Henry Marten, vice-provost of Eton. He was an eccentric figure who secreted lumps of sugar in his pocket that he would munch at intervals; he also kept a raven in his study, which occasionally nipped his ear. He taught the princess not only about the kings and queens of England and Britain but also the very fundamentals of constitutional history – the building blocks of how one day she would reign as Queen. The constitutional textbooks, which are kept under lock and key in the College Library at Eton, are marked throughout with Elizabeth's painstaking annotations, a premonition of the punctilious constitutional monarch who would later be such a diligent reader of her government red boxes.

Her parents did what they felt they could to allow Elizabeth to mix with other girls of her age, to feel that she was part of the world outside palace walls. The 1st Buckingham Palace Guide Company was formed (with a brownie pack for Margaret, who was too young to be a guide) as a substitute for the princesses going out to school, although as a social leveller it was of limited value. As one member recalled: "They were all dukes' daughters and Mountbattens – it wasn't at all democratic." The other girls, who turned up for the first meeting in their best party frocks and white gloves, with nannies and governesses in tow, were expected to curtsy to the princesses.

While Elizabeth enjoyed the fun and games of the guides – the team games, the expeditions, the campfires – she was, in contrast with her sister Margaret, the shy, serious one. Margaret was naughty, high-spirited, amusing and dreadfully spoilt; whenever they had company Margaret would soak up all the attention, a state of affairs that Elizabeth was only too happy to encourage. "Oh, it's so much easier when Margaret's there," she would say. "Everybody laughs at what Margaret says."

Her natural reserve, however, did not prevent her from noticing the handsome young cadet who spent the afternoon with them during a visit to the Royal Naval College, Dartmouth, in July 1939. Elizabeth was 13 years old.

There was an outbreak of mumps and chickenpox at the college and it was thought inadvisable for the two princesses to attend chapel with their parents. Cadet Captain Prince Philip of Greece was 18 and was asked by his uncle, Lord Louis Mountbatten – "Uncle Dickie" – who was part of the royal party, to entertain the princesses.

Philip, who had led a peripatetic existence since his family had been exiled from Greece, was not a wholly unknown quantity. He was, like Elizabeth, a great-great-grandchild of Queen Victoria and he had known the British royal family since he was a child, when he took tea at Buckingham Palace with Queen Mary. She reported him as being "a nice little boy with very blue eyes".

Sketchy accounts, and a couple of photographs, remain of what happened that afternoon. Philip joined the girls when they were playing with a children's train set; later they amused themselves by jumping over tennis nets and playing croquet. Crawfie, not necessarily the most reliable of witnesses, recalled: "I thought he showed off a good deal, but the little girls were much impressed. Lilibet said, 'How good he is, Crawfie. How high he can jump.' She never took her eyes off him the whole time. He was quite polite to her, but did not pay her any special attention. He spent a lot of time teasing 'plump little Margaret'."

Their Dartmouth encounter may not have been the first time they met; other accounts have them meeting at a wedding when he was fourteen and she was nine, and they may also have come across each other at the coronation of George VI. And the 18-year-old Philip – good-looking but offhand, according to Crawfie – was hardly likely to have been instantly smitten by a 13-year-old schoolgirl. There seems little doubt, however, that for Elizabeth it was a pivotal moment. Sir John Wheeler-Bennett, in his official biography of George VI – a work commissioned, scrutinised and approved by the Queen – recorded unequivocally: "This was the man with whom Princess Elizabeth had been in love from their first meeting."

The seeds of love may have been sown but serious courtship was still a long way off; the start of war saw to that.

While Philip was serving with the Royal Navy, Elizabeth made her own contribution to the war effort in October 1940 when, aged 14, she made a radio broadcast as part of a series called *Children in Wartime*. Aimed, in the first instance, at the US and Canada, it was addressed to children but designed to pull their parents' heartstrings. "My sister Margaret Rose and I feel so much for you, as we know from experience what it means to be away from those we love most of all," she said in her clear, high voice. The ending was unashamedly corny. "My sister is by my side," she said, "and we are both going to say goodnight to you. Come on, Margaret."

"Goodnight," piped up an even higher voice. "Goodnight and good luck to you all."

Jock Colville, Churchill's private secretary, was embarrassed by the "sloppy sentiment" of it all but his view hardly mattered: the broadcast was a propaganda triumph and the BBC turned it into a bestselling record.

Philip, meanwhile, was having a good war. He saw action in the Mediterranean and was mentioned in dispatches for his role in the Battle of Cape Matapan against the Italian fleet. He found time to write to Elizabeth, however, and she kept his picture on the mantelpiece.

In 1943 he was invited to spend Christmas with the royal family at Windsor Castle, where he watched the annual Windsor family pantomime. "After dinner, and some charades," Sir Alan Lascelles, the King's private secretary, wrote in his diary for Boxing Day, "they rolled back the carpet in the crimson drawing room, turned on the gramophone, and frisked and capered away till near 1am." Crawfie observed: "I have never known Lilibet more animated. There was a sparkle about her none of us had ever seen before."

As the war drew on, and Elizabeth turned 18, she grew increasingly frustrated. Safely sequestered away at Windsor, her social life consisted mainly of enjoying the company of a group of carefully selected young Guards officers. She was scarcely mixing with a broad range of her contemporaries. All too aware of how her friends were engaged in some kind of war work, she longed to get out and "do her bit".

Finally, in spring 1945, her father allowed her to join the Auxiliary Territorial Service and take a course in vehicle maintenance at Aldershot in Hampshire. It was only a three-week course and, instead of sleeping with the other young women in their huts, she was whisked back to Windsor every night. However, she enjoyed the chatty cups of tea with the other girls and learnt how to service an army truck. However brief her stint in the ATS was – only a few months – it gave her a brief taste of freedom and a uniform.

That uniform proved its worth on the night of VE Day (May 8) when Elizabeth and Margaret slipped out of Buckingham Palace with their young Guards officer friends. They walked to the Ritz and back past Hyde Park Corner before joining the crowds outside the palace where everyone was shouting: "We want the King, we want the King." One of the group, Henry Porchester, recalled: "At last they came out on the balcony and we were mixed up in the crowd, no one noticed, no one recognised Princess Elizabeth or Princess Margaret."

By then Philip was already being considered as a serious suitor. In 1944 his uncle, Prince George of Greece, had made a direct approach to George VI, who said that while he liked Philip, he thought Elizabeth was too young. The Queen was not too sure, either, and a list of suitable young men was drawn up. Philip persisted, while Elizabeth had already made up her mind.

When he proposed to her at Balmoral in the summer of 1946 she immediately set about trying to win her father round. It did not take her long, because the King had already been addressing some of the issues raised by the potential match, such as how Prince Philip of Greece should become a British subject. An accommodation was soon reached: the couple could become engaged but it had to remain a secret until after the family's royal tour of South Africa the following spring.

For a woman who was to become the most travelled monarch in history, the sea voyage to Cape Town was the first time she had set foot outside Britain. Once there, Lascelles thought she did well: businesslike, but with a good, healthy sense of fun. "Moreover," he wrote, "when necessary she can take on the old bores with much of her mother's skill, and never spares herself in that exhausting part of royal duty."

On her 21st birthday, which fell towards the end of the tour, she made the radio broadcast to the Empire and the Commonwealth in which she made a dedication that not only captured the imagination of all who heard it, but has come to serve as a distillation of the sense of service and duty that would become such a consistent theme of her reign. "I declare before you all," she said, "that my whole life, whether it be long or short, shall be devoted to your service and the service of our great imperial family to which we all belong."

The Empire would soon be no more but her devotion to duty – which was a response, in part, to the lesson of the Abdication, in which Edward VIII's personal feelings were allowed to override his royal responsibilities – would help to ensure the survival of the Commonwealth in the decades that followed.

Back home, all was set for a royal wedding. Philip had become naturalised – he was now Lieutenant Philip Mountbatten, RN – and in July 1947 their engagement was announced by Buckingham Palace. The King and Queen were delighted; the palace courtiers, less so. Stuffy, snobbish and deeply antipathetic to this rather disrespectful upstart, they would have preferred Elizabeth to have married someone who would have merged more easily into court circles, some English duke rather than a penniless foreign prince. As Lascelles told a friend: "They felt he was rough, ill mannered, uneducated and would probably not be faithful." In the words of John Brabourne, who was married to Philip's cousin Patricia Mountbatten: "They were absolutely bloody to him. They didn't like him, they didn't trust him, and it showed."

Churchill, on the other hand, thought that the wedding provided just the touch of romance that the country needed as it struggled through the bleak postwar years, describing it as "a flash of colour on the hard road we have to travel". If glamour and romance were what was required, that was what the Palace was going to provide. Norman Hartnell, the royal dressmaker, designed a dress fit for a fairytale princess, of ivory silk decorated with pearls arranged as roses of York, entwined with ears of corn embroidered in crystal. He liked to tell the story of how his manager was stopped at customs after a buying trip to the US and was asked if he had anything to declare. "Yes," he said, "ten thousand pearls for the wedding dress of Princess Elizabeth."

Wedding presents came from all over the world, from the magnificent – a thoroughbred filly from the Aga Khan and a hunting lodge from the people of Kenya – to the comical, a turkey sent by a woman in Brooklyn, because "they have nothing to eat in England". Mahatma Gandhi, at Mountbatten's suggestion, gave a woven cotton tray-cloth that he had made himself and which Queen Mary – no friend of the Indian independence leader – chose to believe was a loincloth. "Such an indelicate gift . . . what a horrible thing," she said.

Although anti-German feeling meant that none of Philip's three sisters, all of whom had German husbands, was invited, the occasion was notable for attracting a splendid array of European royalty. They were entertained in style, with a succession of dinners and parties at St James's Palace and Buckingham Palace. "An Indian rajah became uncontrollably drunk," recorded Colville, "and assaulted the Duke of Devonshire (who was sober)." The King led a riotous conga through the corridors of Buckingham Palace, during which a tiara belonging to Princess Juliana of the Netherlands fell off and had to be stuck back on again. Just before the wedding Philip was granted the style of His Royal Highness and the title Duke of Edinburgh.

On the morning of the wedding – November 20, 1947 – it took Hartnell and his team an hour and ten minutes to fit the dress and 15ft train. However, for all the meticulous planning there were still the traditional last-minute panics that enliven any wedding: the tiara given to Queen Elizabeth by Queen Mary, and now lent to the young bride, snapped and had to be repaired. A further crisis ensued when the princess realised that the double strand of pearls that her parents had given her as a wedding present were half a mile away at St James's Palace with the other gifts. Colville, newly appointed as her private secretary, was dispatched to get them by commandeering the nearest car. Throwing open the door of a royal Daimler, he shouted "To St James's Palace!" to the chauffeur, only to be confronted by an elderly figure, resplendent with orders and decorations, getting out. "You seem to be in a hurry, young man," said King Haakon VII of Norway. "By all means have my car, but do let me get out first."

Inside the abbey, the Archbishop of York told the congregation of 2,000 – the men in uniforms and morning suits, the women in full-length dresses with long white gloves and tiaras – that the service was "in all essentials exactly the same as it would have been for any cottager who might be married this afternoon in some small country church in a remote village in the Dales". Arguable, perhaps, but in one respect at least it was like any other wedding; during the signing of the register the King and Queen were so moved that they were close to tears. As the King told the archbishop: "It is a far more moving thing to give your daughter away than to be married yourself."

After the wedding breakfast the couple were pelted with rose petals by the family as they set off in an open carriage to Waterloo Station. Susan, the princess's favourite corgi, travelled with them, snuggled under a blanket; on arriving at Waterloo she stole the show by tumbling out first in a shower of rose petals.

The procession through Westminster Abbey after the wedding ceremony. The occasion was attended by many heads of state, as well as leading British politicians including Winston Churchill, 1947.

They began their honeymoon at Broadlands, the Mountbattens' Hampshire home, where the phone rang off the hook and royal enthusiasts and newspaper photographers laid siege to the house. There was more peace at Birkhall on the Balmoral estate, where they spent the second half of their honeymoon, warmed by log fires and surrounded by deep snow.

The months and years that followed were good times. When they returned from Scotland, Colville noted in his diary: "She was looking very happy, and, as a result of three weeks of matrimony, suddenly a woman instead of a girl. He also seemed happy, but a shade querulous, which is, I think, in his character."

As a couple they seemed compatible on every level. Sarah Bradford, whose biography of the Queen is arguably the most authoritative portrait of her life, wrote: "Elizabeth was physically passionate and very much in love with her husband." Even if Philip tended more to coolness than passion, he loved and – crucially – respected her.

Yet while unimpeachably supportive and attentive, he was also a domineering figure. In the early days of their marriage, before she had the authority of the sovereign and before she had learnt how to deal with his overbearing ways, they had their moments. He had no compunction about publicly telling the future queen not to be "such a bloody fool". Once, while driving with Lord Mountbatten, Philip was going even faster than usual, causing Elizabeth to draw in her breath. "Do that once more," he told her, "and I'll put you out!" When they arrived, Mountbatten asked her why she had not told Philip that he was driving too fast. "But didn't you hear him?" she said. "He said he'd put me out."

Three months after the wedding she became pregnant. They had been due to move into Sunninghill Park, next to Windsor Great Park, but that burnt down so instead they rented a relatively modest country house, Windlesham Moor, in Surrey. Clarence House, their London home, was in desperate need of refurbishment and they stayed first in Kensington Palace, then Buckingham Palace, before finally moving into Clarence House 18 months after the wedding.

A visit to Paris in the late spring of 1948, her first foreign tour as a newly married princess, was a huge success. The French were struck by her beauty and the quality of her accent, but the warmth of the welcome had its basis in a more fundamental appeal: with her fresh-faced allure, her handsome Viking-looking husband and, once it became publicly known, her forthcoming baby, she was increasingly being seen as a symbol of new era, a beacon of hope as Britain and the rest of Europe emerged all too slowly from the austerity of the aftermath of war.

Behind palace walls small revolutions were taking place too. The King at first insisted that the home secretary should be present at his grandchild's birth, just as his predecessor had been there for the princess's arrival 22 years earlier. Some courtiers thought it was time to do away with this ancient custom but the King demurred until it was pointed out that all the dominions should also have the right to have representatives present, meaning that there might be seven ministers hanging around in the corridor outside her bedroom. He backed down and the Palace announced that it was ending an "archaic custom".

Prince Charles was born in the evening of November 14, 1948; Philip, who was playing squash with Mike Parker, his old Australian shipmate from the war who was now his private secretary, had to be fetched to come and see his new child. Elizabeth was enchanted with her son – she liked his hands in particular, "fine, with long fingers" – but it was not long before mother and child had the first of many separations. First it was illness – she caught measles and it was thought best that they should be apart – then Malta.

Philip had been posted to the Mediterranean fleet in the autumn of 1949 and she went to join him, leaving Charles to spend his second Christmas with his grandparents at Sandringham. Elizabeth, it seemed, could not be accused of being excessively maternal, which may merely have reflected the expectations of her upbringing, but hers was an approach that would lead to painful accusations later in life when Charles laid bare his feelings about his upbringing. He, meanwhile, was forming a close bond with his grandmother, which would become one of the most important relationships of his life.

Princess Elizabeth and the Duke of Edinburgh at the Villa Guardamangia in Malta, 1949.

In the first colour photograph of Princess Anne, taken in 1951, Elizabeth is holding her daughter, and Philip is carrying Prince Charles.

Malta, where Elizabeth stayed for three periods between 1949 and 1951, offered some of the happiest times in her life. For the first time she was able to do all those ordinary things that other people take for granted – to swim in the sea, to go for picnics, to drive a car around the streets, even to do her shopping with her own money. She went to the hairdresser and spent time with the other naval wives – and did not seem to miss Charles at all.

While in Malta she became pregnant again and returned to England to give birth to Princess Anne, later known as the Princess Royal, who was born at Clarence House on August 15, 1950. That Christmas Charles and his sister went to Sandringham while their mother returned to Malta.

While Elizabeth was starting her own family Crawfie, the governess who had devoted 16 years of her life to the two princesses, had married and retired from royal service. Egged on by her acquisitive husband, she signed a lucrative deal to write a book, *The Little Princesses*, which would be serialised in the US magazine *Ladies' Home Journal*. It was harmless, sugary stuff, but the royal family never forgave what they saw as a terrible betrayal. "Doing a Crawfie", as it became known, was one of the ultimate royal sins and neither Elizabeth nor Margaret could even bear to have her name mentioned in their presence. When one visitor forgot, it prompted a sneer of frightening disdain from Margaret: "Crawfie? She snaked."

Elizabeth and Philip's final return from Malta was prompted by the declining health of the King. He had cancer diagnosed – not that the word was used in public – and a lung was removed; the operation was successful, but his doctor knew he did not have long. Elizabeth and Philip stepped in to take the place of the King and Queen on a tour of Canada and the US. It was only a moderate success; the Canadian press decided that she often looked distracted or bored. "Why doesn't she smile more?" they asked.

The following January the couple set off for a tour that was due to take them to Australia and New Zealand, taking in Kenya on the way. The King came to see them off at Heathrow. Margaret MacDonald, by now the princess's dresser, said he told her, "Look after the princess for me, Bobo," and that she had never before seen him so upset at parting from her.

George VI died in his sleep at Sandringham on February 6, 1952; Elizabeth became queen while sitting on the platform of Treetops Hotel in Kenya, watching the animals at a salt-lick from the branches of a giant fig tree. The news took some hours to reach her, by which time she and Philip had returned to Sagana Lodge, their wedding present from the people of Kenya.

Mike Parker, who had been alerted by telephone, broke the news to Philip. "He looked as if you'd dropped half the world on him," Parker recalled. "I never felt so sorry for anyone in all my life."

Philip told his wife. "He took her up to the garden," Parker said, "and they walked slowly up and down the lawn while he talked and talked and talked to her."

Martin Charteris, who had replaced Colville as her private secretary, found the new Queen sitting at her desk writing letters of apology for the cancellation of the tour. She was "very composed, absolute master of her fate", he recalled. A slight flush on her face was the only sign of emotion. "What are you going to call yourself?" he asked. "My own name, of course – what else?" she replied.

On the flight home there was little talk, other than Charteris briefing the Queen on what to expect on arrival. One observer recalled that once or twice she left her seat and when she returned looked as if she had been crying. At Heathrow, Churchill was the first to greet her, but was so overcome with emotion that he could not speak. At the meeting of the accession council at St James's Palace she read the formal declaration of sovereignty to the assembled privy counsellors, and then said: "My heart is too full for me to say more to you today than that I shall always work as my father did . . ." Outside, in the car with Philip, she broke down and sobbed.

In the period of change that followed politicians seized on the accession of this young woman – she was still only 25 when she became Queen – as the dawning of a new "Elizabethan age". Churchill hoped for "a golden age of art and letters" and a time of "true and lasting peace". For others optimism came less easily. Her mother, now styled Queen Elizabeth the Queen Mother, and widowed earlier than she had expected, not only felt the grief at the loss of her husband, but found it hard to cope with the reversal of status between her and her daughter. Philip saw his naval career come to an abrupt end as he was transformed from being a man with a promising future to someone whose existence consisted of walking forever in the shadow of his wife.

The discomfort he felt in being sentenced to play second fiddle for the rest of his life was painfully highlighted by the business of the family name. Word reached the Palace that Lord Mountbatten – the ever-thrusting Uncle Dickie – had been boasting that "the house of Mountbatten now reigned". Queen Mary was outraged, the cabinet was furious, and Philip's tactless if well-argued attempts to put his case infuriated them still further. He told friends: "I am the only man in the country not allowed to give his name to his children."

After a fierce row the Queen was prevailed upon to issue a declaration saying that the family would continue to be known as the House of Windsor. For Philip it was nothing less than a slap in the face, and he took it hard. "I'm nothing but a bloody amoeba," he exploded. The episode demonstrated what would become ever more apparent during the many years of her reign, that there was a natural conservatism to the Queen, allied to a tendency to go with the guidance offered by her advisers. During the preparations for the Coronation – which, because of all the work involved in organising such a spectacle, to say nothing of the timetabling of the official guests, would not be held until June 1953 – the suggestion was mooted that the ceremony should be broadcast on the fledgling medium of television.

The Queen was firmly against. A fundamentally shy woman, not only was she worried that any mishaps would be transmitted live – and here memories were fresh of the litany of foul-ups that had bedevilled her father's coronation – but she also felt that certain elements of the ceremony, such as her anointment and the taking of Holy Communion, were sacred and private. When the decision was made public, the press were up in arms, although wiser newspaper editors took care not to hold the Queen responsible for what they viewed as a reactionary decision, but attributed blame instead to her advisers. After an avalanche of protest the Queen agreed to a compromise: the television cameras would be allowed into the abbey but there would be no close-ups and no filming of the more sacred moments.

While the Queen remained distrustful of television – her Christmas broadcast would not be televised until 1957 – a precedent had been set: she had shown that, faced with overwhelming public opposition, she was capable of changing direction. Regal concessions would be made again at various flashpoints in her reign – the Windsor fire in 1992, the death of Diana, Princess of Wales, in 1997 – but the pattern was set in 1953.

The week of the Coronation was wet and windy but that did not stop half a million people turning out by the evening before to secure their place by the side of the road. The sense of celebration was enhanced by the news, published in *The Times*, that a Commonwealth team of climbers had just conquered the highest mountain in the world. As the Daily Express captured it in a famous front-page headline: "All This – And Everest Too!"

Indeed, it was a day rich with Commonwealth reminders. The Queen wore a dress of white satin, embroidered by Hartnell – at her suggestion – with symbols of the Commonwealth countries: the lotus flower of Ceylon, the wattle of Australia and the wheat and jute of Pakistan, as well as the English rose, the Scottish thistle and the Welsh leek. In the procession down The Mall to the abbey, no one captured the imagination of the crowd quite so successfully as Queen Salote of Tonga, an enormous figure who cheerfully ignored the rain as she rode along in her open carriage.

The Queen returning to the palace after her Coronation at Westminster Abbey on June 2, 1953, wearing the Imperial State Crown and carrying the Orb and Sceptre, followed by Prince Philip.

For the Queen, the solemn ceremony was an affirmation of the vow of service that she had given on her 21st birthday. For those who watched, it was a spectacle, a celebration of national sovereignty, a romantic parade, even a last great imperial display. And for the broadcasters and newsreel companies it was a show whose popularity broke all records. In the US and Canada nearly 100 million people are said to have watched the Coronation on television, making it the top-rated production of the year. The mass media had discovered the unmatched power of royalty, especially young, glamorous royalty, and it was a lesson that they would never forget.

The Coronation also had one other, unforeseen consequence. Margaret was seen to brush – "with a tender hand", no less – some fluff from the lapel of Group Captain Peter Townsend, George VI's former equerry who was then employed by the Queen Mother as master of her household. This immediately fired gossip about a romance and the New York press ran the story the next day. It took another 11 days before *The Sunday People* in Britain reported that the overseas press were saying that Margaret "is in love with a divorced man and that she wishes to marry him".

The bitter saga that ensued, which ended three years later with Margaret deciding to give up Townsend rather than her royal status, can be seen with the benefit of hindsight to show how much attitudes have changed since then. It is also revealing about the Queen. Although sympathetic, she was advised by Churchill and Lascelles, her private secretary, that marriage was out of the question. When Margaret turned 25 she could marry without the Queen's consent but would still have to get parliamentary approval, which was unlikely to be forthcoming.

With the Queen Mother typically simply refusing to discuss the matter, the Queen – who believed, probably correctly, that marriage to Townsend would end in disaster – thought Margaret should make up her own mind but refused to go so far as to tell her so. Instead, she avoided the issue. From the best of motives she was unable to be cruel to be kind and failed to take the tough decisions when they were needed. It would not be the last time the public dimension of her family's private life would end up causing great personal unhappiness.

Notwithstanding the criticism of the Townsend affair directed at the Palace, the early years of the reign were characterised by the great sense of optimism that surrounded the young Queen. Churchill, who when she first acceded to the throne feared that he would never be able to relate to her because she was "only a child", was soon smitten. He would turn up for his weekly audiences in a frock coat and top hat looking positively jaunty, and over time his half-hour meetings would stretch to up to an hour and a half. Asked once what they talked about, he replied: "Oh, mostly racing."

If Churchill was more than a little bit in love with the Queen, he was not the only one. "The world's sweetheart," one American financier called her, and in doing so did no more than give voice to popular sentiment. When she and Philip embarked at the end of 1953 on a six-month, 43,000-mile tour of the Commonwealth, taking in everywhere from Bermuda to the Cocos Islands, and including a three-month sojourn in Australia and New Zealand, she was greeted everywhere with an extraordinary wave of adulation. In Australia it was estimated that three quarters of the population came out to see her; in New Zealand she was welcomed by the Maori as "the rare White Heron of the Single Flight".

Such a mammoth tour – the like of which had not been seen before, and would not be seen again – was an endless ordeal of speeches and banquets and troop inspections, during which she struggled, unsuccessfully, to keep a smile on her face at all times. "Isn't she looking cross?" people would say, disappointed that she was not as delighted to see them as they were to see her. That did not mean, however, that she was not capable of seeing the comical side of it all. On one occasion she had the rest of the royal party in stitches when she performed her own interpretation of the haka in evening dress, complete with grunts and exaggerated gestures. Charles and Anne, of course, stayed at home, although they did come out to visit their parents during a stopover at Tobruk, in Libya; a formal handshake from Charles for his mother in public, and no hugs until they were in private.

At home the Queen was already proving herself to be an assiduous constitutional monarch. Like her father – and unlike her uncle, Edward VIII – she made a point of reading thoroughly her government red boxes and would enjoy catching out ministers who might have skimped their official briefs. Churchill, who became somewhat lazy in his later years, fell foul of this; so too did Harold Wilson, who was furious with himself to be caught out on his first audience. After that they got on very well and on at least one occasion he was asked to stay for drinks. "The Queen never reads a book," said one of her private secretaries, "but when it comes to state papers she is a very quick and absorbent reader – doesn't miss a thing. She impresses all the prime ministers."

Despite her hard work and professionalism, Britain was changing, along with its place in the world, and it was the Suez crisis that brought this message home. Britain's bungled attempt to recapture the Suez Canal in autumn 1956, just over two months after it had been seized by Egypt, dealt the country's national standing a blow from which it would not quickly recover. However, it was the political ramifications that would lead to questions being asked about the role of the Queen.

When Sir Anthony Eden resigned the following January, the Conservative Party set about replacing its leader by commissioning an elder statesman, the Marquess of Salisbury – "Bobbety", a man known for his inability to pronounce his Rs – to take soundings. The choice was between RA Butler, known as Rab, and Harold Macmillan, prompting Salisbury's famous question to members of the cabinet: "Well, which is it? Wab or Hawold?" The Hawolds had it, by an overwhelming majority, but the newspapers, who preferred Wab, were outraged at what they felt was an establishment fix. And the suspicion was that Elizabeth was guilty of naivety in allowing herself to be talked into supporting the chosen candidate of the aristocratic ruling class. This may have been unfair – it is hard to see what she could have done without being accused of meddling in politics – but it reflected a growing feeling in the country that the old school-tie network had had its way for too long.

*In June 1954, the housing minister Harold Macmillan accompanied the Queen
to an exhibition on Oxford Street.*

An incendiary article by a young peer, Lord Altrincham, in the periodical *The National and English Review*, not only laid into her courtiers – "the 'tweedy' sort", he said, who had failed to move with the times – but also criticised the Queen herself. Her speeches were "prim little sermons" and her style of speaking "a pain in the neck". Laying the blame on her entourage rather than the Queen herself, he wrote: "The personality conveyed by the utterances which are put into her mouth is that of a priggish schoolgirl, captain of the hockey team, a prefect and a recent candidate for confirmation." The Queen was furious. She had, according to one source, already been planning to get rid of one outdated palace custom, that of debutantes being presented at court, but kept it going for one more year just to show that she was not going to bow to Altrincham.

For all the uproar, more progressive voices within the Palace realised that there was something in what Altrincham had said. He was invited for a private meeting with Charteris, the Queen's assistant private secretary, who 30 years later would tell Altrincham during a political meeting at Eton: "You did a great service to the monarchy and I'm glad to say so publicly."

Philip was a significant force driving the slow but steady modernisation of the monarchy, such as the lunches that the Queen would hold at Buckingham Palace – initially confined to establishment figures, but later to include actors, writers and sports personalities – but he also became the focus of unwelcome gossip. During 1956 he embarked, accompanied by Mike Parker, on a four-month tour of the outlying territories of the Commonwealth on the Royal Yacht *Britannia*. An expensive, not to say indulgent, expedition that seems hardly credible now, it was almost at an end when the press got hold of the story that Parker's wife was suing him for divorce. That, and the fact that Philip was away for so long, gave the US papers the excuse they needed to start digging into the rumours surrounding Philip's marriage.

It was not the first time that the press had linked Philip with another woman: the gossip columnists had already indulged in speculation about the duke and Pat Kirkwood, the musical star. This time the allegation was that Philip had enjoyed regular assignations with a woman at the Soho flat of his friend Baron, the society photographer who was the linchpin of the mildly louche Thursday Club, whose members would meet for lunch at Wheeler's in Soho and tell risqué stories. Goaded by such headlines as "Report Queen, Duke in rift over Party Girl" the Queen instructed her press secretary to issue a statement denying that there was any such rift, which merely provided the papers with the ammunition for yet more unhelpful headlines.

The fuss soon settled down, but the questions never fully went away. While Philip would defend himself against charges of infidelity by pointing out how he was permanently saddled with his police bodyguards, there was no doubt that he enjoyed the company of close female friends, such as Lady Romsey, who was married to Lord Mountbatten's grandson and with whom he used to enjoy carriage driving.

Sacha Abercorn, another close friend of Philip, said that theirs was a friendship of ideas. "I did not go to bed with him," she told Gyles Brandreth, the writer and broadcaster. "I can understand why people might have thought it, but it didn't happen . . . he isn't like that . . . he needs a playmate and someone to share his intellectual pursuits." As for the Queen, Abercorn said: "She gives him a lot of leeway. Her father told her, 'Remember, he's a sailor. They come in on the tide'."

Her reference to Philip's intellectual pursuits highlighted one of the key differences between him and Elizabeth: that while he had a restless curiosity about the world of ideas, she had little time for intellectuals or writers. Daphne du Maurier, whose husband "Boy" Browning worked for Philip during the early years of the Queen's reign, found him quick and easy to talk to, but Elizabeth heavy going. She was good on politics and world affairs and lit up whenever the conversation turned to horses, but struggled when it came to literary matters.

As a child, Elizabeth told Horace Smith, her riding master, that when she grew up she would like to be "a lady living in the country, with lots of dogs and horses", and she always appeared happiest when she was at Balmoral or Sandringham, surrounded by her animals.

That passion for country pursuits came with a deep knowledge too, whether it was for gun dogs or thoroughbreds. Her grandfather, George V, named a bay filly Lilibet after her and her most successful horse was Aureole, who won 11 of his 14 races. The story goes that on the morning of the Coronation, just as she was about to leave Buckingham Palace for Westminster Abbey, a lady-in-waiting asked her if everything was all right. Oh yes, replied the Queen: she had just heard from Aureole's trainer, and everything had gone well in his preparation for the Derby (which took place four days later, with Aureole coming second, the Queen's best result in the one classic that she never won).

Queen Elizabeth II patting her horse, Aureole, after it came in first at the Royal Ascot race meeting on Ascot Heath, Berkshire, 1954.

For all their differences, the Queen and the Duke of Edinburgh enjoyed a relationship in which they gave love and respect, and a measure of freedom, and received in return the support that, for her at least, was the only way she could carry out her role. That was not to say that their marriage was not prey to the tensions that afflict every relationship. In Australia, during their Commonwealth tour of 1953-54, a local camera crew was waiting to shoot some footage of the Queen when Philip ran out of the chalet where the couple were staying, with a pair of tennis shoes and a racket flying after him. The Queen appeared a moment later, shouting at Philip to come back. Eventually, she dragged him into the chalet and the door was slammed. Later, she was charm itself to the camera crew. "I'm sorry for that little interlude but, as you know, it happens in every marriage," she said. "Now, what would you like me to do?"

Beyond exposing the fact that the Windsors experienced the same marital storms as anyone else, the episode also reflected the changing dynamic of the relationship between the monarchy and the media. The cameraman dutifully handed over his film of the row to the Queen's press secretary; indeed, on the same tour a government delegation arrived at the Australian *Daily Mirror* demanding the surrender of a photograph of the Duke of Edinburgh with a drink in his hand. Fifteen years later, in 1969, the royal family would allow the cameras in to film a family barbecue, and in 1994 the Prince of Wales would be on television confessing adultery.

After a decade of marriage the Queen and Philip decided to have more children. It took two or three years of trying, from when Philip returned from his four-month cruise on *Britannia*, but when she became pregnant the couple were overjoyed. The Queen thought that it was extraordinary, after so long. It did, however, mean cancelling a planned visit to Ghana. Charteris was dispatched to Accra to break the news to Dr Kwame Nkrumah, the country's leader, who told him: "If you had told me my mother was dead, you couldn't have given me a greater shock. I have put all my personal happiness in it [the royal tour]." He got over his disappointment, and when the Queen finally visited Ghana, Charteris said, she "twisted him round her little finger".

Her pregnancy was not the only sign that the marriage was on a sound footing. In February 1960 the Queen announced a compromise on the delicate question of the family name: from now on, she said, while the royal family would continue to be known as the House of Windsor, descendants who were not a prince or princess – in other words, the ones who would actually use a surname – would bear the name Mountbatten-Windsor. The decision was plainly the result of much heart-searching; Macmillan, who talked it through with the Queen at Sandringham, told friends that "it was the first time he had seen the Queen in tears".

Prince Andrew was born on February 19, 1960; Prince Edward followed four years later, on March 10, 1964. It was while pregnant with Edward that the Queen found herself once more at the centre of a constitutional row over the leadership of the Conservative Party.

As he contemplated his resignation in the aftermath of the Profumo scandal, Macmillan was in hospital, but determined to ensure that his rival, Rab Butler, did not get the job. The Queen was equally determined not to repeat the mistakes of the last time. After she visited Macmillan in hospital, when he gave her the name of Alec Douglas-Home, 14th Earl of Home, she did not give Douglas-Home the job at once, but invited him to see if he could form a government commanding a Commons majority.

This he was able to do, and he was confirmed as prime minister. Yet it did not remove the suspicion that it had been another stitch-up by the grouse-shooting classes: as Tony Benn put it, becoming a Tory prime minister was not so much a question of first past the post, but first past the Palace. Once more the Queen had been made to look as if she were capable of siding only with the Tory party's tweedy tendency.

If her role in Macmillan's succession is still the subject of debate among constitutional historians, her slow response to the Aberfan disaster was more of a puzzle. In 1966, 144 people were killed, 116 of them children, when a slagheap collapsed on the Welsh village. At a time that called out for a spontaneous gesture, the Queen did not visit the scene for eight days. It was, supposedly, because she did not want to interrupt the rescue and rehabilitation work; it may also have been because she did not like to intrude on private grief or to show raw emotion in public. Charteris would describe her as a woman whose skill was to know when to say no, rather than to come up with ideas. "She's got superb negative judgment," he said. "But she's weak at initiating policy, so others have to plant the ideas in her head." Later she would admit privately that her delay in visiting Aberfan was a mistake and she wished she had gone earlier.

In other ways, and particularly overseas, she was increasingly confident in her role, and the globetrotting monarch spent the Fifties and Sixties on a series of groundbreaking foreign tours. On her visit to India in 1961, when she was the first British monarch to visit the country since George V half a century earlier, more than a million Indians turned out in New Delhi to welcome her. The effect, however, was spoilt somewhat by Philip shooting a tiger on a hunt, which went down badly at home. The visit later that year to Ghana, postponed from when she was pregnant with Andrew, was overshadowed by Nkrumah's ever more anti-western stance as well as bomb attacks in Accra. However, the tour was a great success: the country's neo-Marxist *Evening News* said that all Ghana had been moved by this "most modest, loveable of Sovereigns" and called her "the world's greatest Socialist Monarch in history". A state visit to Germany in 1965, the first by the royal family since before the First World War, caused the Queen much anxiety beforehand but, thanks to the warm reception she received, turned out to be a far more enjoyable experience than she had anticipated.

Others were less enjoyable. A visit to the UK in 1963 by King Paul of Greece and his wife, Queen Frederica, which was controversial because of the Greek government's civil rights record as well as Frederica's alleged Nazi sympathies, led to the crowd booing not only the Greek king and queen but also the British royal family. Elizabeth's tour to Canada the following year, which drew protests in Quebec, was one of the most difficult that she had undertaken. In a conciliatory speech she stated that a "dynamic state should not fear to reassess its political philosophy" and remarked that it was not surprising that "an agreement worked out 100 years ago does not necessarily meet all the needs of the present". She received a better welcome in Ottawa, but it was admitted that the tour had "undoubtedly given rise to more controversy and anxiety, in Canada and Britain, than any before it".

On the domestic front they were now a family of six. While Elizabeth was accused of lacking maternal feeling – a criticism highlighted by Charles's complaints about his upbringing, which would surface in Jonathan Dimbleby's biography in 1994 – she was overjoyed to have Andrew and Edward, and was more relaxed with them than she ever was with Charles and Anne. "Goodness what fun it is to have a baby in the house again!" she told a friend after Edward was born. Her favourite night of the week was "Mabel's night off", when the nanny was out and she could put the boys to bed herself.

Her instinct was to protect her family's privacy, but as the decade progressed it became apparent that something needed to be done about the royal family's public image, which was seen as fusty and out of date. Persuaded by the Mountbattens and William Heseltine, her bright new Australian press secretary, the Queen agreed to let the cameras in. *Royal Family*, which was first shown in July 1969, was a revolution in the way that the royals were depicted on screen. Until then it was unheard of to see the Queen working on a speech with her private secretary, let alone relaxing with her family on a picnic beside Loch Muick at Balmoral.

The results revealed the naturalness and spontaneity of a woman who, in formal contexts, came across as stiff and remote. Among the footage of state visits and private audiences there were shots of Charles bicycling in a London street, Philip grilling steaks on the barbecue, and the family sitting around the lunch table telling not particularly funny stories. They were, in other words, just another family. Since then commentators have argued about whether it was wise, to borrow Bagehot's phrase, to let daylight in upon magic, and whether the film created the public appetite for insight into the personal lives of the royal family, thus leading to the flood of prurient and intrusive media coverage that would be unleashed little more than a decade later with the arrival on the scene of Lady Diana Spencer. Most likely it would have happened anyway.

There were other changes afoot in the way that the royal family revealed themselves to the public. Charles's investiture as Prince of Wales at Caernarfon Castle on July 1, 1969, a colourful, television-friendly pageant that commanded enormous viewer ratings, demonstrated new ways of presenting the royal family in a media age, which emboldened them to more colourful showmanship in later parades and jubilees. The following year in New Zealand, with crowds larger than expected, the Queen and the Duke of Edinburgh took an apparently unscheduled and casual walk along the street, shaking hands and chatting with the public. Such performances are commonplace now, but then they were a radical departure from accepted practice. A reporter borrowed a word previously used to describe the wanderings of Australian Aborigines in the bush: the walkabout was born.

In 1972 the Duke of Windsor died. The lasting rift between the abdicated king and the royal family had been an issue throughout the Queen's reign. He had not been invited to the Coronation, because it was felt constitutionally inappropriate, although there was a reconciliation in 1965 when the Queen visited her uncle while he was in London for an eye operation. Ten days before he died she visited him at his home in the Bois de Boulogne, in Paris. According to his doctor there were tears in her eyes as she left; she had been moved by the meeting, which brought back memories of her own father. After a funeral at St George's Chapel, Windsor, the duke was buried at Frogmore, where he would be joined by the duchess 14 years later.

The Silver Jubilee in 1977 was a surprising success, as indeed was every jubilee that followed, suggesting that, whatever the media might say, and whatever day-to-day grumbles people might have had about the royals, there was an underlying respect and affection for the Queen that was remarkably resilient. With the economy in the doldrums, the government did not want to spend any money and the Queen – modest as ever – did not want any overblown celebrations, but in the event the commemorations in June led to a spontaneous outpouring of popular feeling. There were flags, bonfires and street parties. The Queen was quite taken aback at it all. "She could not believe that people had that much affection for her as a person, and she was embarrassed and at the same time terribly touched by it all," said her domestic chaplain.

After Edward Heath, whom the Queen found hard work, and James Callaghan (who astutely observed that what the Queen offered her prime ministers was "friendliness but not friendship"), the election of Margaret Thatcher as prime minister in 1979 brought new challenges. In many ways the two women could not have been more different. The Queen was naturally conservative and a countrywoman at heart, while Thatcher was a radical and did not have a country bone in her body; bracing walks at Balmoral were something she endured rather than enjoyed. Their greatest divergence of opinion was over the Commonwealth, an institution the Queen had inherited from her father and to which she gave her utmost dedication. Thatcher was far from keen.

While the Queen never took sides publicly, according to Sir Sonny Ramphal, the secretary-general of the Commonwealth, there was no doubt where she stood on the divisive issues of the time: Rhodesia and apartheid. In 1979, when Britain was unpopular with black African leaders because of its failure to help to bring about a solution to the fighting in Rhodesia, the Commonwealth summit in Lusaka, in Zambia, looked set to be a disaster; yet somehow it was a success, with an accord that would lead to the foundation of Zimbabwe.

Behind the scenes the Queen, who knew many of the African leaders of old, is considered by many to have played a part. In Ben Pimlott's analysis she was an emollient, a figure outside politics who had an understanding of both sides of the argument. "She talked to Mrs Thatcher and to [Kenneth] Kaunda [the Zambian president]," said Ramphal. "The fact that she was there made it happen. Kaunda felt that he'd have let her down a little if he hadn't pulled it off."

Her differences with Thatcher emerged in spectacular fashion with a *Sunday Times* story that said the Queen was dismayed by Thatcher's policies over a wide range of issues, including the crisis in the Commonwealth over South Africa. She found the prime minister's approach to be "uncaring, confrontational and divisive", the paper said. The source for the story was Michael Shea, the palace press secretary, but whether he went too far in representing an anti-Thatcher view, or whether *The Sunday Times* exaggerated his remarks, will remain a subject for conjecture. Either way, the Queen stood by him. The evidence, however – the Order of Merit that the Queen conferred on Thatcher after her resignation, and the fact that she attended her funeral – implies that the Queen had more time for the first of her three female prime ministers than a casual reading of events would suggest.

One embarrassment that Thatcher could have lived without was Michael Fagan's break-in at Buckingham Palace. Fagan, a 33-year-old man with schizophrenia, had managed to bypass security and get into the Queen's bedroom on the morning of July 9, 1982. Unable to raise help, the Queen talked to him sympathetically for ten minutes until he asked for a cigarette, which she used as an excuse to get him out into the corridor. The maid, who had been vacuuming in the next room, exclaimed: "Bloody 'ell, Ma'am, what's 'e doing 'ere?" Moments later the police arrived. "Oh come on, get a bloody move on," said the Queen, as one officer paused to straighten his tie.

The previous year there had been another security scare when a youth in the crowd at Trooping the Colour fired six shots – which turned out to be blanks – at the Queen as she rode by. Showing remarkable coolness under fire, she ducked, patted her horse Burmese, and rode on.

The Queen and the Royal Family on board the Spirit of Chartwell leading a flotilla of more than 1,000 boats down the Thames. The pageant was the climax of her Diamond Jubilee celebrations in 2012.

The Queen had already been on the throne for nine years when the woman who would have a greater impact on the monarchy than anyone since Wallis Simpson was born. When, in the second half of 1980, Charles began to take Lady Diana Spencer seriously as a possible bride, his parents were concerned that he was in danger of dithering for too long. The Queen voiced her feelings to a friend, but said nothing to Charles; Philip had to tell his son that he had to propose or end the relationship.

Diana's sense of alienation began when she moved into Buckingham Palace before the wedding. She felt lost, overawed and ignored. However much truth there was in that – palace insiders said they went out of their way to help her – she and the Queen had little in common. As the marriage deteriorated and a partisan war developed between Charles and Diana's camps, the Queen and her advisers stood accused of failing to understand the glamorous and widely adored princess, of cold-shouldering her and squandering an asset that had given the royal family its first international superstar.

At pains not to take sides, the Queen felt that she could not interfere to help to save her son's marriage; later, when the couple's relationship neared the point of no return, it was the Duke of Edinburgh who took the initiative. After a meeting between Elizabeth and Philip and Charles and Diana at Windsor, which went some way towards clearing the air but failed to achieve anything substantial, Philip began in 1992 writing a series of letters to Diana that were frank, direct, but sympathetic and more than aware of Charles's faults. They achieved little, other perhaps than to upset the eternally fragile Diana. Eventually there was nothing more that Elizabeth and Philip could do, although the Queen made one last attempt to hold things together by persuading Diana and Charles to go ahead with a joint visit to South Korea. It was not a good idea. The tour was a disaster, with the couple clearly unable to bear the sight of each other, which merely provided the press with more ways to write about the collapsing marriage. Shortly after their return Charles decided there was no future in their marriage and asked his wife for a legal separation. It was announced on December 9, 1992.

Before that, there was worse to come. On November 20, Philip and Elizabeth's 45th wedding anniversary, a fire broke out at Windsor Castle when a restorer's lamp set a curtain alight. Within hours the fire was out of control, badly damaging St George's Hall, the state dining room and three drawing rooms, and destroying several roofs. The Queen was devastated; not only was Windsor the symbol of the monarchy, it was her childhood home and the place she loved more than anywhere else.

Four days later she gave a speech at Guildhall, London. The lunch was to celebrate her 40th year on the throne, but instead it came to mark everything that had gone wrong in that most disastrous of years for the royal family. As well as the Windsor fire and the breakdown of Charles and Diana's marriage, there had been the divorce of Princess Anne and Captain Mark Phillips, the separation of the Duke and Duchess of York (whose marriage had collapsed amid a series of lurid exposés in the press, including photographs of the duchess having her toes sucked by John Bryan, her "financial adviser"), and the publication of a recorded phone conversation between Diana and her lover James Gilbey (the "Squidgy" tape). "1992 is not a year on which I shall look back with undiluted pleasure," the Queen said. "In the words of one of my more sympathetic correspondents, it has turned out to be an annus horribilis." *The Sun* translated it as "One's Bum Year".

Two days after that John Major, the prime minister, announced that the Queen and the Prince of Wales would pay income tax and that the Queen would – out of her income from the Duchy of Lancaster – reimburse the civil list annuities received by the Princess Royal, Prince Andrew, Prince Edward, Princess Margaret and Princess Alice, Duchess of Gloucester.

Controversy over the money allotted for the royal family had been a running sore for decades. When she was still Princess Elizabeth there was resentment about how much she would get from the government on her marriage to Philip. In 1969 he had blundered on US television when he announced – during negotiations between the Palace and the government that until then had been conducted in secret – that the royal finances were so tight that he might have to give up polo.

Major's statement was a woeful public relations own goal. It gave the impression that the Queen had been panicked into paying income tax by the furious public reaction to the announcement by Peter Brooke, the heritage secretary, that public money would be used for the repair of Windsor Castle, estimated at £60 million. In fact, negotiations about tax had been going on behind the scenes for many months, but it suggested that she had caved in to a tabloid campaign.

The broader point was still true, however; her decision to agree to remove the anomaly over income tax was indeed a response to public criticism of the monarchy and the way it was financed. It was just a question of timing. The following spring Major announced that the restoration of Windsor Castle would not be funded by public money, but mainly by opening parts of Buckingham Palace to the public.

The question of money would continue to bedevil her reign. In the 1980s under Lord Airlie, the lord chamberlain, the Queen instigated an overhaul of the way that the Palace and its finances were run, which saved millions of pounds. Gratitude, however, was in short supply. Most of the money-saving measures met with the approval of the Queen, a naturally thrifty person. However, the axing of *Britannia* in 1997 was a decision motivated by politics as much as money and the Queen was seen to dab a tear from her eye as it was decommissioned. In 2012 George Osborne, as chancellor, in an attempt to stave off the political rows that invariably surrounded the civil list, introduced the sovereign grant. The rows, of course, continued.

The aftermath of Charles and Diana's separation left Elizabeth depressed by the family situation and its repercussions. She and Philip would wonder – as indeed would many others – to what extent they were to blame for the failure of not only one but three of their children's marriages. "What did we do wrong?" they would ask friends. There were more unpleasant surprises in store. From the Queen's point of view the 1994 television film that Charles made with Jonathan Dimbleby, in which he confessed to adultery with Camilla Parker Bowles (but not "until the marriage had irretrievably broken down"), was bad enough; Dimbleby's biography was worse. Charles, through Dimbleby, laid much of the blame on the way his parents had brought him up. His mother had been remote, and his father a bully. Both had been "unable or unwilling to proffer . . . the affection and appreciation" that he craved.

Relations between Charles and his mother had not been easy for a long time. Over the years their relationship became ever more distant, partly because they were not living under the same roof, and partly because of a failure to communicate on any deep, personal level. They exchanged social pleasantries and dealt with family business, but little more than that. As Charles gained confidence, the rift between his household and the Queen's grew wider. "Though the prince disguised his growing resentment – except from his intimates," Dimbleby wrote, "he was quick to detect any apparent slight from the Queen's officials and began resolutely to distance himself from them."

However cool things were between Elizabeth and her eldest son, the accusations about his upbringing still came as a bitter blow. She put a brave face on it. Her other children, however, were outraged by what Charles had said about their parents in public and told him so.

Diana's interview on *Panorama*, in which among other things she cast doubt on whether Charles was fit to be king, was the spur that finally persuaded the Queen that the situation had become so intolerable she had to take the initiative. Just before Christmas 1995 she wrote to Diana and Charles advising them that they should begin divorce proceedings. The marriage formally came to an end on August 28, 1996.

Almost exactly a year later Diana was killed in a car crash in Paris. In the week that followed, a spontaneous public outpouring of grief for Diana was accompanied by a groundswell of opinion that the Queen, who was at Balmoral with Charles, William and Harry when the news broke, had somehow failed to respond in a way that the press and public deemed appropriate.

Far removed from the emotional turmoil in London, the Queen, who had no precedent to fall back on, was at first unsure how to react. Her natural desire was to protect her grandsons, which meant keeping them at Balmoral, away from the limelight. Her default position was to do what she always did at times of stress – to rely on tradition and routine to see her through.

On the morning of Diana's death, therefore, the family went to morning service at Crathie Kirk as normal. The boys were told that they did not have to attend, but decided they would because it was preferable to being left behind. A perfectly sensible decision, from the Balmoral perspective; to the outside world it came across as the Windsors in typically cold-hearted fashion forcing the boys out in public. There was more outrage over the flag: why was the Union Jack not flying at half-mast over Buckingham Palace? The answer, that the royal standard is the only flag that flies over the palace, and then only when the sovereign is present – and never at half-mast – did not satisfy anyone. A compromise was reached: the Union Jack would fly over the palace at half-mast.

It was the Queen herself who became the focus of criticism. Why was she hiding away at Balmoral? Why had she not spoken in public about Diana's death? As the week wore on, she realised that she had to change tack.

On Friday, the day before Diana's funeral, she flew to London where, highly nervous about the reception she would get from the crowd, she left her car with Philip to look at the sea of flowers outside the palace. But it was all right: the crowd broke into applause and a young girl handed her some flowers. "Would you like me to place them for you?" the Queen asked. "No, your majesty. These are for you," came the reply.

That evening she spoke live on television of Diana as "an exceptional and gifted human being" who she "admired and respected". In a conclusion that carried a surprising note of humility the Queen added: "I, for one, believe that there are lessons to be drawn from her life and from the extraordinary and moving reaction to her death." It was a touching and sincere broadcast that struck the right note and won over most of her critics, but – as the reaction to Earl Spencer's barbed words about the royal family at the funeral made clear – the Queen knew that the royal family would once more have to change.

Slowly, the family's stock began to rise. The Queen continued with her daily duties. Contrary to the impression that Diana might have given, Charles proved himself publicly what he had always been privately: a good father to William and Harry.

The death of Princess Margaret in February 2002 and the Queen Mother the next month evoked great sympathy for the Queen. The celebrations for the Golden Jubilee that year showed that the royal ship was back on course and in 2005, after years when it seemed uncertain that Camilla Parker Bowles would ever be welcomed into the royal family, she and Charles married at Windsor. The Queen did not attend the ceremony at Guildhall, but afterwards spoke warmly at the reception at Windsor Castle. In a wry reference to the day's other big event, the Grand National, she said: "Having cleared Becher's Brook and the Chair, the happy couple are now in the winner's enclosure."

One of the most significant factors in the revival of the family's popularity was the arrival of Kate Middleton. William and Harry had already shown a new informality in their way of approaching their royal responsibilities, but it was William's marriage to the daughter of a middle-class couple from Berkshire that showed how the royal family was moving away from its traditional, hidebound assumptions – not least about breeding, in every sense of the word – and adapting to the 21st century.

Kate was welcomed into – and protected by – the royal family in a way that Diana never was. So were her parents: while the Spencers had long moved in royal circles, the Middletons were not the sort of people who would have received a social invitation from the royals. Now they were invited to Balmoral, where they were seen flat on their stomachs in the heather being coached in the art of stalking by a ghillie, and Sandringham. The Queen is said to have liked the cosy atmosphere at the Cambridges' family home, where the duchess's mother, Carole, has been a regular fixture.

Three generations of the British Royal Family – Queen Elizabeth II, Prince Charles and Prince William – pose for a photograph at Clarence House to mark the 50th anniversary of her Coronation, 2003.

The marriage of Prince Harry to Meghan Markle in May 2018 marked another shift in the royal family's attitude and relationship to the outside world. A couple of generations earlier the monarchy had an existential crisis over a proposed marriage to an American divorcee: some 80 years later, when Harry's American divorcée was also an actress of mixed race, the royal family – and the nation – took it all in their stride. The day before the wedding the Queen was spotted being driven through Windsor with Meghan's beagle, Guy, sitting next to her in the back of the car. Markle, now the Duchess of Sussex, was part of the family, and so was her dog.

When Elizabeth acceded to the throne she was Queen of 32 nations. By the end of the 20th century that number had been whittled down to 16. In 1999 Australia – where memories still rankled over how Sir John Kerr, the governor-general and the Queen's representative, had sacked Gough Whitlam as prime minister in 1975 – held a referendum on whether the country should become a republic. The voters, unimpressed with the alternatives on offer, voted to keep the monarchy. By the time the Queen and the Duke of Edinburgh paid their last, triumphant visit there in 2011, republicanism was well off the political agenda.

In 2014, when the referendum on whether Scotland should leave the United Kingdom was proving to be a closer-fought battle than anticipated, the Queen made a delicately worded but deliberate last-minute intervention to save the Union by allowing herself to be heard telling a member of the public that she hoped people would "think very carefully about the future".

One of the great successes of her reign was the 2011 state visit to Ireland, the first visit there by any British monarch since 1911. In previous years she had undertaken tours to many countries for the first time – to China and to Russia, as well as the first visit to South Africa under majority rule – but it was Britain's nearest neighbour that eluded her longest.

From the wreath-laying at the Garden of Remembrance in Dublin, where she bowed her head at the memorial to those who had died fighting for Irish independence, to her speech at Dublin Castle on Anglo-Irish relations, where she offered a few words in Gaelic, the visit went better than even the most optimistic officials had dared to hope.

So, too, did the Diamond Jubilee the next year, when a series of visits she undertook to almost every corner of the country inspired people to come out in their thousands to greet her, often in spite of inclement weather. The absence through illness of the Duke of Edinburgh from the concert at Buckingham Palace and the service at St Paul's was a reminder of how much the Queen relied on the man who had been steadfastly by her side for more than 60 years. He had developed a bladder infection the day after spending several hours on the Thames for the river pageant, a miserably cold, wet and blustery occasion in which the Queen, in characteristically dutiful form, stood on the deck of the royal barge for the length of its voyage, ignoring the thrones that had been constructed for the occasion.

Always modest and respectful of her place in history, when she became the country's longest-serving monarch in September 2015, the Queen wanted above all for the day to pass without fuss. It was not to be, but she made her feelings known when she said in a short speech that the anniversary was not one to which she had aspired. "Inevitably a long life can pass by many milestones," she said. "My own is no exception."

Another milestone followed in 2016, when she celebrated her 90th birthday. There was a picnic for her charities in The Mall organised by her grandson Peter Phillips, an event at which everyone did their best not to mind that it poured with rain for almost the entire duration; a horse pageant at Windsor, which was probably the Queen's idea of a perfect evening's entertainment; and a service at St Paul's that was notable for its lack of gushing tributes. As one close to the Queen remarked: "Every single thing was as she would want it, no emotion."

In the midst of duty, tradition and service, she was still capable of surprises. A reminder of that was given during the celebrations for her Platinum Jubilee when she appeared in a film having tea with Paddington Bear, and produced a marmalade sandwich from her handbag.

If the Queen's job was to ensure stability – to be there when, in Yeats's words, "things fall apart, the centre cannot hold" – she was sorely tested in the latter years of her reign. In August 2019 Boris Johnson, manoeuvring his way towards Brexit, asked the Queen to prorogue parliament, only to have his decision overturned by the Supreme Court. Then the royal family suffered successive blows when the Duke of York and then the Duke and Duchess of Sussex stepped down as working royals.

Andrew's departure was the result of a calamitous interview with the BBC's *Newsnight* about his friendship with the convicted paedophile Jeffrey Epstein. Two months later the Sussexes, bruised by their battles with the media and frustrated by their dealings with the Palace, announced that they were stepping away from royal duties and going to live in North America. In both cases the Queen's decisive – not to say ruthless – action served as a reminder of the strength and will with which she had kept the monarchy in good health over eight decades of radical change.

During the coronavirus pandemic she spent much of her time at Windsor Castle in isolation with Philip. Her national broadcast during the first lockdown, with its message of "we'll meet again", was welcomed as a timely and well-judged boost to the country's morale. Later she encouraged people to have the vaccine by announcing when she had had it herself.

Philip's death in April 2021 after 73 years of marriage was a blow she managed with her customary stoicism. She cut a lonely figure at his socially-distanced funeral, but was back at work within a fortnight of his passing. That was her promise, a life dedicated to service. She kept her word.

Her Majesty Queen Elizabeth II was born on April 21, 1926. She died on September 8, 2022, aged 96.

Queen is laid to rest with splendour and pageantry

It was the longest of farewells, a day of history marked with tears and marching bands, timeless ceremony and an outpouring of emotion during which tens of thousands lined the streets to catch their last glimpse of the Queen.

It began with the splendour of a state funeral at Westminster Abbey, where world leaders gathered to pay respect to the monarch who had acceded to the throne before most of them were born.

It ended eight hours later when, in an intimate ceremony away from the cameras, her family saw her buried alongside the Duke of Edinburgh in a crypt at St George's Chapel, Windsor.

A day that had been planned for decades began with the Queen's coffin being taken from Westminster Hall, where she lay in state for four days, to the abbey, borne on a gun carriage drawn by a total of 142 naval ratings.

The coffin was draped with the Royal Standard and topped with the instruments of state: the Imperial State Crown, the orb and the sceptre. Next to them sat a wreath of flowers picked from the gardens at Buckingham Palace, Clarence House and Highgrove.

Tucked among the flowers was a handwritten message from the King, which said: "In loving and devoted memory. Charles R." The coffin was followed on foot by the King and other royal family members, including his sons the Prince of Wales and Duke of Sussex.

Inside the abbey they were joined by the two youngest members of the royal family ever to join a royal funeral procession, Prince George, nine, and Princess Charlotte, seven.

At the funeral service more than 2,000 mourners filled the abbey, including some 200 heads of state, foreign royals and other overseas dignitaries. Most were bussed to the abbey. President Biden of the US was one of the few granted permission to take his own transport.

They were joined by emergency workers, members of the late Queen's household and holders of the George Cross and Victoria Cross.

In the abbey David Hoyle, the Dean of Westminster, spoke of the Queen's sense of duty and "her long life of selfless service". He said: "With gratitude we remember her unswerving commitment to a high calling over so many years as Queen and Head of the Commonwealth. With admiration we recall her lifelong sense of duty and dedication to her people."

The Archbishop of Canterbury said she had touched "a multitude" of lives in her 70-year reign.

The service ended with the Last Post and two minutes' silence before the sovereign's piper played a lament.

Then, carried by a bearer party from the Queen's Company, 1st Battalion Grenadier Guards, the coffin was moved out to the gun carriage to be taken in procession to Wellington Arch.

The security challenge of hosting so many of the world's VIPs meant that the area around Westminster Abbey was completely closed to the public.

Instead the crowds, which had been gathering for days in the hope of a glimpse of the procession, lined Whitehall, The Mall and Hyde Park Corner.

As the King and other royals followed on foot, their faces stoical, some members of the public were in tears. They were mourning the only monarch most of them had known.

The procession was led by Canadian Mounties followed by NHS workers including May Parsons, who administered the first Covid-19 vaccine in 2020.

The procession was formed of seven groups and made its way around Parliament Square, past a guard of honour comprising army, navy and RAF personnel. In total, more than 3,000 members of the military took part.

At Wellington Arch the coffin was transferred to the state hearse to be driven to Windsor for the committal service at St George's Chapel. By the time it reached the Long Walk, where thousands more had gathered to see its final journey, the hearse was strewn with flowers thrown by mourners.

As the procession made its way through Windsor Great Park, Terry Pendry, the late Queen's head groom, led out Emma, her fell pony, to see the coffin go past. At Windsor Castle, where the royal family once more formed a procession behind the hearse, there was another poignant moment when two of the Queen's corgis, Muick and Sandy, were brought out.

At the committal service, a far more intimate occasion than the funeral at the abbey, the final ceremony marking the death of the sovereign took place.

At the end of the service the instruments of state were removed from the coffin and placed on the altar as the lord chamberlain broke his wand of office. Along with the camp colour of the Queen's Company, 1st Battalion Grenadier Guards, it was placed on the coffin to be buried with her.

Then, as David Conner, the Dean of Windsor, proclaimed the words "Go forth upon thy journey from this world, O Christian soul", the coffin was slowly lowered into the royal vault.

The service ended with the Garter King of Arms reading the styles and titles of Queen Elizabeth II, a blessing and the singing of the national anthem.

With that, a long day of public ceremonial was over. But for the royal family, there was one last chance to say their farewells.

At 7.30pm, after the coffins of the Queen and the Duke of Edinburgh had been brought up from the Royal Vault, a small private burial ceremony was held in the King George VI Memorial Chapel, attended only by her closest family. There the Queen and her husband of 73 years were buried together, alongside her parents, George VI and Queen Elizabeth the Queen Mother, and her sister Princess Margaret.

The grave is marked with a slab of black marble that is already inscribed with her parents' names. It will now bear the words: Elizabeth II 1926 – 2022.

The Times, September 19, 2022

The royal family and world leaders gather for the state funeral of Queen Elizabeth II at Westminster Abbey, London, on September 19, 2022.

Crowds gather to watch the ceremonial procession travel down the Long Walk, making its final journey to Windsor Castle.

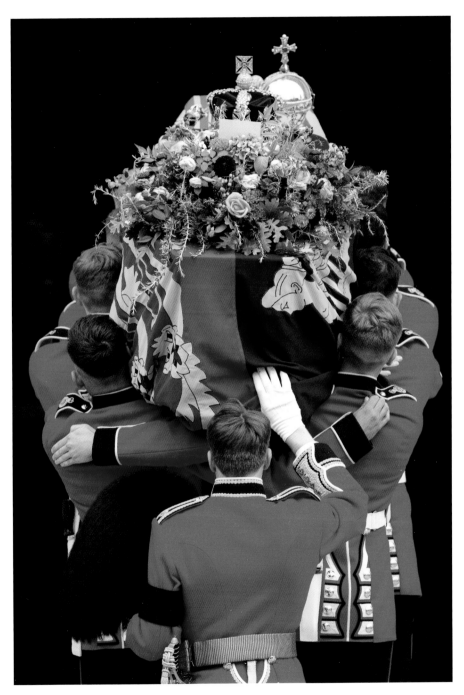

Pallbearers from Queen's Company, 1st Battalion Grenadier Guards, carry the coffin into
St George's Chapel for the committal service.

A HARD ACT TO FOLLOW

by Ben Macintyre

One way to assess the legacy of Britain's longest-reigning monarch is to look back to where her story started. *The Times* of April 21, 1926, carried a very small announcement on page 14, between a report on ructions in the German cabinet and another on the progress of the economy bill: "The Duchess of York was safely delivered of a Princess at 2.40 this morning. Both mother and daughter are doing well." The baby would go on to become Elizabeth II.

Hers was an extraordinary reign, not just for its longevity but for its strange and effective combination of consistency and adaptability, tradition and subtle innovation. She has left the monarchy more secure than many would have predicted, but her very success has left her heirs a problem: she will be a remarkably hard act to follow.

The newspaper on the day of her birth announcement reflected a secure, stratified society, a Britain that was still imperial and colonial; it was complacently and deeply royalist, confident in its collective identity. Reporting on the royal family was demure, discreet and, above all, deferential.

The Britain Elizabeth came to rule in 1952 was still recognisable as the one she had been born into. The news of her accession reached her in Kenya, then still firmly under British rule despite rumblings of rebellion. She had every reason to expect that she would rule in much the same way as her father and grandfather. It did not turn out that way.

As she observed in her Golden Jubilee speech of 2002: "Since 1952 I have witnessed the transformation of the international landscape ... matched by no less rapid developments at home, in the devolved shape of our nation, in the structure of society, in technology and communications, in our work and in the way we live."

The London of 1952 still had trams and smog. Churchill was still prime minister, and British troops were still fighting in Korea. The mathematician

Alan Turing was forced to undergo hormone treatment to avoid prison for his homosexuality. Britain remained an intensely traditional, old-fashioned realm with an enigma. She may have ruled for longer than any other British monarch, but few of her subjects can remember anything she said. In the intrusive, fast-moving 20th and early 21st centuries, she proved that distance could be a source of royal strength.

So what does the legacy of Elizabeth II, and the way monarchy evolved under her, indicate about the coming reigns of Charles III, William V and, eventually, George VII? If the Elizabethan age is anything to go by (and it is), the monarchy of the future will be smaller, older, cannier, funnier, more reticent and micromanaged; underdressed in private moments and lavish in public ceremonial; more informal but not more intimate. Royalty will appear more middle class, while being nothing of the sort.

It will be run on business lines. Under Elizabeth, monarchy just about broke even, but that has set up expectations of royal solvency; henceforth, it will have to show stakeholders a clear cultural profit.

The problems in Elizabeth's reign came when modernity collided with what the Victorian writer Walter Bagehot called the mystery and magic of "the charm of royalty". The family has suffered the sort of problems that afflict most other families: bereavement, failed marriages, younger members behaving badly. Yet whereas the deference of the first half of the century would have ensured such events were treated with decorum and euphemism, the insatiable curiosity of the second half of the 20th century and the start of the 21st meant that those moments have been scrutinised with brutal intensity.

As a consequence, the modern monarchy has become adept at presentational skills and the alchemy of public relations in a way that would have been unthinkable a generation ago. The key strategy (almost a mission statement) is now to enable the monarchy to appear more like the rest of us, while maintaining its mystery. Catherine, the Princess of Wales, is the perfect embodiment of this approach, being university educated, well dressed, decorous and part of a middle-class family that appears almost quintessentially unremarkable and unthreatening. She has brilliantly absorbed the lessons of Elizabeth II's reign: smile, laugh even, put everyone at ease, say nothing controversial, and wear jeans as easily as a tiara.

There are now enough male royal heirs to last a century, and the future kings will have plenty of time to rehearse. To judge from the longevity of the Windsor bloodline, and based on actuarial calculations, William will be in his sixties before he wears the crown; George is likely to be even older.

When she succeeded her father, the details of the life of 25-year-old Elizabeth were almost unknown to the British public. Even her nanny, Marion Crawford, who supposedly "told all" in 1950, told very little. Our future monarchs will be exceptionally well known to us by the time they succeed. What they do before becoming kings will matter just as much as what they do on the throne.

Older monarchs may have experience and maturity; the disadvantage is that with age come opinions. Queen Elizabeth resolutely avoided intruding on politics; Charles, as Prince of Wales, has shown no such self-restraint, insisting, in his own words, that he is "determined not to be confined to cutting ribbons". Perhaps the central question of the monarchy's future is the extent to which the institution can afford to become political. Too outspoken, and it risks fomenting division and controversy; too reticent, and it risks irrelevance.

The British monarchy has survived by giving the impression that it remains a still point in a moving world, a bastion of tradition but adaptable with it. Elizabeth maintained that illusion. Yet her successors will be required to be moving points in a world that is itself moving at staggering speed, transformed by global influences on British society, economic transition, social and ethnic migrations and radical institutional reform. Our national identity, so static and predictable at the time of Elizabeth's accession, is now in violent flux.

We are long past the time when monarchy could expect to be loved and revered simply for being, for the accident of breeding. It is a cliché to talk of a monarchy "winning" the respect of its people, but Elizabeth's reign demonstrated just how easily even a popular queen can lose monarchy's popular purchase – and win it again. This is a judgmental, demanding and overachieving age.

The next generation of monarchs will have to do something more admirable than the run-of-the-mill royal activity: write something, explore something, prove something or achieve something. Some are born great, some have greatness thrust upon them; the next generation of royals will have to work harder for greatness than any before it.

Queen Elizabeth may come to be seen as the most successful monarch in British history, if success is measured by problems overcome, stability maintained and succession secured. She has left a monarchy that is still recognisable, but also transformed, and certain to change yet more. Her subtle force of personality kept the royal ship afloat; for her heirs, royal rule will also be a test of character and resolve.

Perhaps the most important aspect of Elizabeth's legacy will be the ethic of hard work, deep in old age. To live up to this shining example, her heirs will have to work their royal socks off.

King Charles III during his proclamation as King on September 10, 2022 in London.

IMAGE CREDITS

pp.6–7: Max Mumby/Indigo
p.11: Max Mumby/Indigo
p.15: George Rinhart
p.18: Universal History Archive
p.19: Paul Popper/Popperfoto
p.22: Bob Thomas/Popperfoto
p.23: Bettmann
pp.24–25: Lisa Sheridan / Stringer
p.26: Paul Popper/Popperfoto
p.27: Lisa Sheridan / Stringer
p.29: Print Collector
p.31: Popperfoto
pp.32–33: Paul Popper/Popperfoto
p.34: Popperfoto
pp.36–37: Popperfoto
p.40: Bettmann
p.41: Lisa Sheridan / Stringer
p.43: Central Press / Stringer
pp.44–45: Mirrorpix
p.49: A. J. O'Brien / Stringer
p.50: Popperfoto
p.51: Popperfoto
p.53: Topical Press Agency / Stringer
p.55: Bert Hardy / Stringer
pp.56–57: Picture Post / Stringer
p.59: Uncredited/AP/Shutterstock
p.61: ANL/Daily Herald/Shutterstock
p.62: ANL/Shutterstock
p.63: Everett/Shutterstock
p.65: Uncredited/AP/Shutterstock
p.67: John Rider-Rider/AP/Shutterstock
p.69: Everett/Shutterstock
p.71: Lichfield
p.72: Tim Graham
p.75: Anwar Hussein
p.76: Anwar Hussein
p.77: Lichfield
p.78(t): Mirrorpix
p.78(b): Hulton Archive / Stringer
p.79: Tim Graham
p.83: - / Getty
p.86: Lisa Sheridan / Stringer
p.87: Hulton Deutsch
p.89: ADRIAN DENNIS / Staff
p.92(t): Mirrorpix
p.92(b): Keystone / Stringer
p.93: Universal History Archive
p.95: Popperfoto
p.99: Universal History Archive
p.108: Shutterstock
p.109: PA Images / Alamy Stock Photo
p.110: PA Images / Alamy Stock Photo
p.111(t): PA Images / Alamy Stock Photo
p.111(b): Paul Popper/Popperfoto
p.112: ADRIAN DENNIS / Stringer
p.113: PA Images / Alamy Stock Photo
p.114: Keystone-France
p.115: Nat Jag
p.117: REUTERS / Alamy Stock Photo
p.118(t): Ken Goff
p.118(b): JOHN STILLWELL / Stringer
p.119: Anwar Hussein
p.122(t): David Levenson
p.122(b): Anwar Hussein
p.123(t): PAUL J. RICHARDS / Staff
p.123(b): WPA Pool / Pool
p.124(t): Bettmann

p.124(b): Georges De Keerle
p.125: Peter Macdiarmid / Staff
p.127: Dan Kitwood / Staff
p.128: RON BELL
p.129(t): UniversalImagesGroup
p.129(b): Rolls Press/Popperfoto
p.130(t): Win McNamee / Staff
p.130(b): Keystone-France
p.131: Popperfoto
p.134(t): Fox Photos / Stringer
p.134(b): PA Images / Alamy Stock Photo
p.135: Anwar Hussein
p.136(t): Anwar Hussein
p.136(b): POOL / Pool
p.137(t): Popperfoto
p.137(b): Popperfoto
p.140: Anwar Hussein
p.141: Anwar Hussein
p.147: Mirrorpix
p.149: THOMAS COEX
p.151: Evening Standard / Stringer
pp.154–155: AFP / Stringer
p.157: Kirstin Sinclair / Stringer
p.158: Anwar Hussein
p.160(l): Shutterstock
p.160(c): Tim Graham
p.160(r): Samir Hussein
p.161(l): Max Mumby/Indigo
p.161(c): Samir Hussein
p.161(r): Max Mumby/Indigo
p.162(l): David Levenson
p.162(c): Keystone / Stringer
p.162(r): Max Mumby/Indigo
p.163(l): Max Mumby/Indigo
p.163(c): Tim Graham
p.163(r): Samir Hussein
p.164(tl): Reginald Davis/Shutterstock
p.164(tr): Lichfield
p.164(bl): Serge Lemoine / Stringer
p.164(br): Tim Graham
p.165(tl): David Levenson
p.165(tr): Tim Graham
p.165(bl): Ray Bellisario/Popperfoto
p.165(br): Tim Graham
p.166(l): Lisa Sheridan / Stringer
p.166(c): Tim Graham
p.166(r): David Hartley/Shutterstock
p.167(l): Reginald Davis/Shutterstock
p.167(c): ADRIAN DENNIS / Staff
p.167(r): Tim Graham
p.171: Joan Williams/Shutterstock
p.174: Hulton Archive / Stringer
p.175: WPA Pool / Pool
p.176: Lichfield
p.179(t): Lisa Sheridan / Stringer
p.179(b): Central Press / Stringer
p.180(t): PA Images / Alamy Stock Photo
p.180(b): Today/Shutterstock
p.181: Anwar Hussein
p.184: Kirstin Sinclair
p.186: Central Press / Stringer
p.187: Tim Graham
p.188: Peter Macdiarmid / Staff
p.189: Max Mumby/Indigo
p.195: Lisa Sheridan / Stringer
p.196: Tim Graham
p.197: Trinity Mirror / Mirrorpix / Alamy Stock Photo

p.199: Lisa Sheridan / Stringer
p.200: Keystone Press / Alamy Stock Photo
p.201(t): Fox Photos / Stringer
p.201(b): Bettmann
p.207: Hulton Deutsch
p.208(t): Anwar Hussein
p.208(b): Central Press / Stringer
p.209: PA Images / Alamy Stock Photo
p.211: Princess Diana Archive / Stringer
p.212: Shutterstock
p.213: JOHN STILLWELL / Staff
p.218: Tim Graham
p.219: Tim Graham
pp.222–223: David Levenson
p.225: REUTERS / Alamy Stock Photo
pp.226–227: JOHN STILLWELL / Staff
p.229: Mark Runnacles / Stringer
p.230(t): Anwar Hussein
p.230(b): WPA Pool / Pool
p.231: PHIL NOBLE / Staff
p.234(t): Max Mumby/Indigo
p.234(bl): Chris Jackson / Staff
p.234(br): John Cantile / Stringer
p.235: Abaca Press / Alamy Stock Photo
p.238(i): Mark Cuthbert
p.238(ii): Max Mumby/Indigo
p.238(iii): Yui Muk/AP/Shutterstock
p.238(iv): Yui Muk/AP/Shutterstock
p.239(i): Robin Utrecht/Shutterstock
p.239(ii): Tim Rooke / Shutterstock
p.239(iii): DAVID HARTLEY/Shutterstock
p.239(iv): Tim Rooke/Shutterstock
p.242(t): Tim Graham
p.242(b): ALASTAIR GRANT / Stringer
p.243(t): UK Press
p.243(b): Mark Cuthbert
p.245: Ray Tang/Shutterstock
p.246(l): Ray Tang/Shutterstock
p.246(r): David Fisher/Shutterstock
p.247: Tim Rooke/Shutterstock
p.252: WPA Pool / Pool
p.253: PA Images / Alamy Stock Photo
p.258: Pool/Max Mumby
p.259: WPA Pool / Pool
p.260: Max Mumby/Indigo
p.261: Max Mumby/Indigo
p.272: Popperfoto
pp.274–275: Hulton Deutsch
pp.284–285: Fox Photos / Stringer
p.288: Hulton Archive / Stringer
p.289: Keystone / Stringer
pp.294–295: Topical Press Agency / Stringer
p.299: Jimmy Sime / Stringer
p.302: Reg Speller / Stringer
pp.306–307: Hulton Archive / Stringer
pp.312–313: Jeff J Mitchell / Staff
p.320: Anwar Hussein
p.327: WPA Pool / Pool
p.328: WPA Pool / Pool
p.329: Max Mumby/Indigo
pp.330–331: JONATHAN BRADY
p.335: WPA Pool / Pool
Hard cover images:
Front: Lisa Sheridan / Stringer – *Princess Elizabeth at Buckingham Palace, July 1946.*
Back: Bettmann – *Princess Elizabeth on board the HMS Vanguard, February 1947.*